Inspired Girls International
P.O. Box 5713
Sherman Oaks, CA 91413

Visit us online: www.inspiredgirlsonline.com

Printed in the United States of America

This book is available for bulk purchases. Contact us to learn about available discounts. info@inspiredgirlsonline.com

Inspired Girls International is a subsidiary of Inspired Life Media Group.

ISBN: 978-1-450-78698-0
Cover design by Scott Mosher

The Legacy Letters

30 Women Address the Next Generation

Lisa Nicole Bell

DEDICATION

This book is dedicated to every woman and girl who insists on pursuing her dreams.

Gratitude

God: For the vision, the courage, the stamina, and the clarity...I'm grateful.

Mom + Dad: Your love, support, and listening ears are priceless. I love you dearly and will be eternally grateful for what you have been to me. We'll do our victory dance after you read this!

Contributing Writers: Each of you is infinitely amazing. I had a vision at 3 A.M. that has now become a tangible blueprint for becoming a woman who's smart, confident and strong. Thank you for enrolling in my vision and selflessly sharing your story. Your transparency on the page inspires me.

Supporters + Fans: Thank you. I don't take your support and loyalty lightly. My intention is always pure: I create projects to in humanity and move the social agenda forward. Thank you for your implicit nod to the value of this work.

Clients: You inspire me to be, do and have the best. Thank you for trusting me to empower you.

Special Acknowledgements

Dr. Jaelline Jaffe

Lisa Elia

Arel Moodie

Taylor Aviles

Lisa Steadman

Jennifer Lawhead

Wadooah Wali

Carrie Fox

Table of Contents
Letter from the Editor

From the Editor's Pen

One night I awoke from a dream about a girl who appeared to be lost in a maze. She kept crying out for help, but no one reached out to help her. She eventually gave up and sat sobbing on the ground, unable to find her way. A week later, I had a dream of myself sitting in a room with the teenage girl from the maze. This girl seemed like a stranger – her appearance and disposition were very different than my own. I was attempting to have a conversation with her. She started out rolling her eyes at me and looking at the floor. As I continued, her eyes eventually met mine. The girl I was speaking to was me.

I woke up in tears because the conversation was heavy. I sat up, scribbled "Conversation with younger self" on my bedside notepad, and attempted to get back to sleep.
I cried myself to sleep that night. It wasn't a sad cry; it was a cleansing cry. The kind where you just "let it all out" even if you can't articulate what all "it" entails. I sat in meditation the morning after,

attempting to make sense of what this meant for me when I heard a small, still voice say, "It's not for you. It's for someone else." I knew that meant I was preparing to give birth to something bigger than me. I took a deep breath, realizing that I had to get out of the way and allow this to manifest in whatever form it was supposed to. I immediately put a brief together and approached thirty of the most amazing women I knew. Every one of them said yes to my proposal.

What you are reading is a gift to women and girls that came through me. I consider this work a love letter to the next generation of feminine leaders. I believe that the societal and economic issues of our generation and the next will require that young women be equipped to seize opportunities. This anthology and its ancillary pieces are intended to offer a sober reflection on the challenge of becoming a woman and a priceless guide to reducing life's learning curves.

Like a mother who's just given birth, I'm proud of what this project is and can become. I have fed it and nursed it. Now it's time for it to exist outside of me and be a blessing to you.

With gratitude,

Lisa Nicole Bell

Sharon Lechter

Entrepreneur + Co-author,
Rich Dad, Poor Dad
book series

Dear Sharon,

As I thought about what to share with you, I looked back over my life and realized how much I have to be grateful for. To change anything that has happened to me would mean that I would be a different person today. Along my life's journey, however, I have learned a few lessons which would have served me well at your age.

Today, you have a blank canvas on which to build your future. Allow yourself to dream about the life you want to live. There are limitless possibilities. As you welcome each day, do so with eager anticipation. Laugh more, smile more and don't take yourself too seriously. There will be those days that seem like eternities, and others that pass with the blink of an eye.

Your future will be created by the decisions you make along the way. Take ownership of those decisions.

Along life's path we all tend to create limitations for ourselves, often without even realizing it. Endeavor to watch your own vocabulary when speaking to others but also, and even more importantly, when talking to yourself. Commit to never say "if only I", "I can't" or "I'll try." Instead say "when I", "I can" or "I will" and your life will be fulfilled in ways beyond your imagination.

As you go through life, you will make mistakes. See them as stepping stones along your path to success. Mistakes are how you learn what "not to do" next time. Thomas Edison failed 10,000 times before he discovered the light bulb. He said, "when I" not "if only I." "If only I" means you are dwelling in the past and allowing your failures to define you. You obsess over missed answers on tests or making a mistake and you beat yourself up for days.

As you get older, you will find peace and be able to see your mistakes as learning opportunities. Now I force myself to say, "When I..." and look forward to the future instead of worrying about the past. By simply training yourself to catch yourself when you start to say, "If only I" you will save yourself heartache. Catch yourself...and replace it with "When I."

"I can't" creates a box around you. Do you want to live in a box? I don't think so. Ask yourself, "Why not?" Asking this question led to the life changing decision to leave the corporate accounting profession to live the life of an entrepreneur, and I have never regretted it. By asking yourself, "Why not?" you will open your mind to the possibilities of new life experiences. As a 48 year old, I found myself again saying "I can't" when my husband and I discussed learning to scuba dive. However there was this inner force that made me go through the training, in spite of my "I can't scuba dive" mentality.

What a sense of accomplishment I felt when I succeeded in becoming a certified diver and I truly loved it! Today, I cannot imagine having missed the experiences and thrill of scuba diving all over the world. When faced with a new opportunity I continue to ask myself, "Why not?" It gives me the courage to try new things and experience more of what life has to offer. (Last year I went zip lining in Costa Rica!) As you move forward in your life and find yourself challenged with new opportunities, don't ask "why?" Instead ask yourself "why not?"

When you say the term "I'll try", you are making a half-hearted promise. When you say "I will", you are making a commitment. While I still catch myself the term "I'll try" these days, it usually triggers a smile. I smile because I realize I have just caught once again, and it forces me to challenge myself. I stop and ask myself, "Am I committed or not?" Whether I say, "I'll try to eat better" or "I'll try to exercise", it usually means my heart is not really into whatever the issue is.

Today, when I tell a friend "I will" meet them, they know that they can count on me.

Do you want to be someone others can count on? Pay attention to your vocabulary, not only when you speak to others but also when you speak to your mirror as well. Replace "I'll try" with "I will."

As you start to employ these tools in your life, you will discover a huge fringe benefit. You will be taking more ownership in your life, and your self-confidence will soar. Instead of being influenced by the negativity of others around you, you will become a positive influence for them. You will also find yourself to be more present or "in the moment."

This will allow you to not only listen better but also spot opportunities more quickly. As you become more aware of opportunities around you, you will also be well served to become a master of money instead of a slave to money. Start early by learning how to create money through your own entrepreneurial spirit of creativity.

As you learn to create wealth from these opportunities, you will gain knowledge that few others possess. But be careful of debt - it is the single most dangerous tool that will make you a slave to money for far longer than you can imagine. Your self esteem will soar exponentially as you watch your savings and assets increase.

It is through the power of entrepreneurship that you will find financial success. In addition to the financial freedom, you will discover your true purpose. It will give you more peace, fulfillment and joy than anything else.

Discovering your purpose will give you the ability to give back to others by using your talents, your time and your money to serve others. You will find the greatest joy in life through service to others. All the material possessions in the world do not compare to the feelings that are invoked when you look into the eyes of someone saying "thank you" from the bottom of their heart.

The world would be a much better and joyous place if we all would endeavor to add value to the lives of others each and every day. Today is the first day of the rest of your life. May your life bring you great joy!

Sharon Lechter

Sharon is an entrepreneur, author, philanthropist, educator, international speaker, licensed CPA and mother. She has been a pioneer in developing new technologies to bring education into children's lives in ways that are innovative, challenging and fun, and remains committed to education – particularly financial literacy. In 1989, she joined forces with the inventor of the first electronic 'talking book' and helped him expand the electronic book industry to a multi-million dollar international market. Since 1992, she has dedicated her professional life and directed her entrepreneurial efforts in the creation and distribution of financial education books, games and other experiential learning products.

Aiesha Turman
Filmmaker + Educator

Dear Aiesha,

I need you to know that you are loved and that you always will be. I need you to value your uniqueness, because as you grow into yourself, it will propel you into success, bringing you the joy that you think eludes you. There is absolutely nothing wrong with you, so please stop hiding your body under those baggy clothes. You can't help it if you developed early and remember, anything negative that someone says to you is a reflection of their character, not yours.

And another thing, please stop dumbing yourself down. You are brilliant! You aren't graduating at 16 for nothing. I know you think it makes boys more comfortable when you hide your brilliance, but trust me, the right boys will really like the total you – brains and all.

I know that you desperately want to fit into the box that others have created for you, but don't. It was only after I stopped listening to others and believing that what they wanted for me was best, that I was able to find my place in the world. When that happened, my life took off in directions that I could not have even imagined.

I am now enjoying a life of my own creation and success on my own terms. And finally, I won't warn you of people or places to avoid because it's through all of these experiences that you'll grow into a dynamo!

You are going to face some painful experiences, but it's the choices you make during and after those experiences that will help you develop into an amazing woman, mother and friend whose talents will be used to educate, entertain and get folks thinking.

Love you always,
Aiesha

Aiesha is a Brooklyn-based creative who utilizes traditional and emerging media as tools for investigation into the lives of one of the most marginalized groups in America. Aiesha uses the tools to engage in frank dialogue surrounding the issues of race, class, gender, spirituality and sexual orientation and the roles they play in the lives of Black communities.

ၰၕ

Annamaria Poluha
Wellness Coach

Dear Maria,
People have often described you as wise, insightful and gracious. You are an old soul. What you know today won't be very different than in the future. It's important that you trust what you know and simply go for it! Trust your intuition, and then take that step out into the unknown, even when it's a little scary. Start taking imperfect action; you can always tweak your strategy once in motion.

Your path has been challenging – and you will realize that all those challenges will provide you with the strength and knowledge you need to stand on your own two feet. Know that God puts these challenges into your life and that he is giving you an amazing gift to share with people for the rest of your life.

Trust that you will grow stronger with each challenge and that you will find peace, love and adoration.

In the moments when you don't know how to move forward, trust that there is another side to what you are experiencing right now. There is always a breakthrough to be had – just imagine that you are climbing a mountain and that with each step you are closer to the summit. Once there, you have overcome those challenges that are put in front of you today, and it'll be like they never even existed. You are very strong, and it's your strength and persistence that causes you to reach the summit and never turn back. It's your strength that gives you the tools to live a life of freedom and joy. When you feel that you can't take another step, remember that there is an enormous light at the end of the tunnel. As you are seeking the light, it's also seeking you. You have always been so straightforward and consistent – you never fake anything, you never pretend to be somebody you aren't. You stay grounded and it's this trait that will lead you to create the life you desire. It's this way that will make you the most satisfied.

Every time you notice that you aren't your true self –
that something doesn't feel right - it's OK to simply stop
and reassess. Always connect with your truth, and don't
take anything personally. What might be hurtful today
will be your greatest lesson tomorrow.

From time to time, there are detours in life, and you
might think you are wasting your time. You will learn
that nothing is a waste. Detours will be your biggest opportunities to grow, and they will provide the greatest
tools and insights to you.

You may often feel judged and misunderstood. You may
also feel that people are here to hurt you – know that
each and every person you meet throughout your life
has a specific role. Listen to them, hear their pain, and
resolve it if you can but then move on. You so
desperately want to help, but sometimes you simply
need to let go. Your parents love you deeply. They did
the best they could at that point in their life, and they
are extremely proud of you. Surrender to their love and
the love all of your friends have for you – it is in that
place that you'll find the most happiness.

There are no problems you cannot overcome. Just imagine what you want, see it clearly,
define it thoroughly, and trust that it can be yours!

Love,
Annamaria

ଶ୦ଓଷ

Annamaria Poluha embarked on a journey to make a difference in the field of self-esteem, nutrition, and fitness after her revelation of its tremendous effect on her own life. After a long battle with the aftermath of anorexia, bulimia and excessive exercise disorder, she found the missing threads – the power of nutrition, the philosophy behind blood sugar stabilization and the influence of positive psychology. Annamaria has taught corporate workshops and women's retreats, written for AOLHealth.com, and appeared as health expert on numerous radio programs. She was featured in Fitness Magazine for her victorious battle with bulimia and developswinning strategies in life balance, self-esteem and effectiveness. Annamaria is a master certified nutritionist (IBNFC), certified life coach (CPCC), certifiedpersonal trainer (NASM), and a published writer. Learn more at www.wellnessdynamics.com

ଶ୦ଓଷ

Mandy Hale
Relationship Writer

Dear Mandy,
I can almost picture you as I type this: innocent, idealistic, unsure of yourself and your place in the world, a little timid and insecure, barely tipping the scales at 105 pounds and with big brown eyes rivaled only by the size of your big, beautiful, bleeding heart. Sixteen years later, that heart will be just as big.

There are a few things I'd like to tell you about life, my sweet, youthful doppelganger. Some of them will make you smile, some will make you cry, some might shock you, and some might cause you to want to take a different path when you arrive at the various crossroads mentioned below. would, however, urge you not to. While it is my hope that you will walk these same paths with a little more confidence and self assurance than I did; I still hope you will be brave enough to boldly follow your heart the way I always have – even when it leads you into dark places where you're not sure you want to go.

Here's a secret: Those dark places will only serve to make your inner light shine more brilliantly than it already does. So here goes. Are you ready?

In the year 2000, you will embark upon a five-year journey to not so much as kiss a boy because you have an idealistic; albeit, somewhat misguided plan to wait until your wedding day to kiss again. One day, you will land the job that has been your dream job since you were a little girl – a television producer for Country Music Television! – but it will be taken away just one year later. It won't matter too much, though, because that same year, you will become an aunt, and you will love these two little girls more than you ever thought possible to love anyone, and they will bring you immeasurable joy.

As busy as life gets, spend as much time as you can with Nanny and Grandaddy...and follow through with that plan you always had to interview them about their lives on tape. It will mean the world to you later when both of them are bedridden and unable to share with you all the stories that you forgot to make time to hear the first time around.

One night, you will wander into a bar and meet a boy that will change your life forever. Word of advice: Risk it all...take a shot...throw all caution to the wind, and actually tell this boy how you feel about him, just to see if anything turns out differently this time around. Maybe...just maybe...this time, he'll stay. And if he DOES stay, then maybe you won't begin that relationship in 2008 that will nearly destroy you. Believe it or not, you will willingly see this relationship through to the bitter end; enduring a litany of abusive and unhealthy behaviors, until you are a mere shadow of the woman you used to be. When all is said and done, though; you will be grateful for the pain and for the rain of those lonely two years, because they will transform you into the woman that you are today.

And who is that woman, you ask? She is...The Single Woman.

Your 31st year will be your best year EVER; a year of self discovery and passion and enlightenment in its purest, rawest form. You will finally be settled into your niche in life; you will be surrounded by the best friends of your life; and more than 185,000 people AROUND THE WORLD will care about what you have to say each day. Which reminds me – that prophecy you will receive in church in 2002 about you "speaking into the lives of many young women" might not come true for nearly ten years, but trust me on this one:

It WILL come true. In a BIG WAY. You might not believe me when I tell you this, but an army of strong women, who don't yet know you exist, will allow you to speak wisdom and encouragement into their lives on a daily basis.

Yes, you will finally grasp how to love with every ounce of your being, live life to the last drop, and doggedly pursue the road less traveled in search of your destiny, no matter how many around you choose Easy Street. But...after careful consideration, my young friend, I have decided that maybe I will just let you figure all of these beautiful lessons out on your own. To tell you the future would be to compromise the journey. To tell you would be to forever change the outcome of certain events, thus changing the "Me" that was born from every tear, every laugh, and every heartbreak. Go back and alter even one step along the way, and we would not be who we are today. And though we would almost certainly, at first instinct, choose to save ourselves from the pain, doing would mean we would never experience the gain.

The blessings that came as a result of the lessons. The victory that came as a result of defeat. The break-up call that was really a wake-up call. The agony and the ecstasy of living every moment, facing down the fears and the tears, and coming out on the other side, still standing, stronger and better and more powerful than ever. Do even one thing differently, and we might have become someone else entirely, with some other script, some other dream, some other life.

So, what words of advice do I have for you, Mandy? Smile...lighten up...hum a little in the shower and sing a little in the car. Look up at the stars more and maybe even make a wish on one, and most of all...believe that the wish really could come true. Travel. Walk barefoot in the grass and dance in the rain and pick a dandelion and blow all of its wondrously white fuzzy petals away, as hard as you can. Take more chances. Do more dances.

Dream more and sleep less and laugh until you cry and eat cotton candy simply for the fun of feeling it melt in your mouth. Be brave enough to believe in yellow brick roads and white picket fences and knights in shining armor...of summer days and ice cream trucks and sandcastles and fireflies. The journey, my friend, is not always going to be easy...but it will always, always be worth it. Finally, never stop following your own north star...and always remember that it's okay to be YOU. Simple, human, fallible, wonderful you. See you in sixteen years.

With love,
Mandy

Mandy Hale is affectionately known around the world as "The Single Woman". In one year, Mandy has garnered a massive Twitter following of more than 250,000 people from across the globe and has tweeted her way to being the #3 most
popular Twitter page in Tennessee. Dubbed by many as "the Carrie Bradshaw of Music City," Mandy cuts to the heart of the matter with her inspirational, straight-talking, witty, and often wildly humorous take on love and life. Recently voted a 2011 "Woman of Influence" by the
Nashville Business Journal under the category of Inspiration/ Mentor, Mandy is making a name for herself as the voice of empowerment and
sassiness for single women across the globe.

Erica Nicole

Entrepreneur + Editor-In-Chief, YFS Magazine

Erica Nicole:

I have some things to share with you about life, love, happiness, business, success and your future. Nearly 13 years later, I have traveled the world and grasped a significant truth that will help you on your journey. In fact, it will equip you to live the life you have always imagined.

And it begins with your destiny. You see, you have been assigned a boundless destiny. Your life will ultimately become the sum expression of quality decisions – choose wisely.

Erica, live a life that you are proud of... live a life of fearlessness. Start now, time is fleeting. Fearlessness coupled with faith unlocks the doors to your greatest dream.

Youthfulness often deceives you and traps you with the belief that life is "all about you." Know that you will only step into your God-given destiny when you realize with courage and conviction that your life is in fact – not your own – "it's about others."

Begin today, with the utmost haste, to serve others and ultimately sow into others that which you need. Continue to walk with God – remain in Him and He will remain in you; you cannot do this alone. Apart from Jesus Christ you can do nothing.

In this lifetime, you will overcome great pain and trials which will set the stage for rapid movement into your destiny. Great love is a part of that destiny. Learn to love yourself and operate in love – in all things; without love nothing else works. When it comes to matters of the heart, don't settle for anything less than what God has for you. You have been empowered to fulfill a great destiny – and love is a ministry [purpose and service]. God *will not* send weak ministry to a great destiny.

The difficult circumstances in life and the times of waiting often refine, teach and prepare us for the future responsibilities God has for us. And while this may seem trite, learn to embrace rejection. Rejection is a divine announcement that a person is no longer able to support your destiny and purpose. Throw yourself a going away party and move forward in your purpose. In the end love has no guarantee. Love is an act of faith, and whoever is of little faith is also of little love. The lesson: develop unassailable faith. Have faith in yourself.

Happiness does not exist on the outside – it's a root issue and it starts with you. Cultivate a state of thanksgiving in all that you do. Live your life pursuing your passions every day – try something new, venture into the unfamiliar, embrace knowledge. Every limitation is self-imposed. Don't look for approval from others and stop living from the outside in. Happiness is an inside job.

As in chess, life is played in the mind – not in the hand. Start now and build your vision; entrepreneurship is your passion.

Don't listen to people who aren't where you want to be. Don't spend your life playing it safe… yes, you won't lose anything but you assuredly will not gain anything either. Seek knowledge first. Soar with eagles – you are a born winner. As with life, love and happiness… business is an inside victory. Dream by day, create something from nothing and construct your reality. Make a choice to do what you think you cannot do.

In the end, it seems purposeful to seek success and the outward expression of material wealth. True riches lie in seeking greatness. God prepares great men for great tasks by great trials. There will be no comfort in your growth zone and no growth in your comfort zone. Continue to invite change – be malleable. The greatest loneliness is to live outside of God's perfect will for your life. Seek purpose, not success.

For the future, be quick to forgive and slow to anger. Pick your battles. Know when to invest in others and when it is time to cease. Everything has its season. Never allow inconsistent and vacillating people to take up room in your life.

You have too much destiny within you to let people get in the way. Base your life on purpose – not people. Change your mind, renew your thoughts to align with the word of God and change your world. Be bold, be fearless, forgive often, listen more and never ever stop living your dreams out loud. The world awaits you.

I Love You,
Erica Nicole

PS: The secret to greatness lies in Proverbs 16:3; live it.

As a serial entrepreneur, small business expert, syndicated columnist, national conference speaker, Christian thought-leader and philanthropist, Erica Nicole is a global media & marketing powerhouse. As an accomplished entrepreneur, Erica leads a growing portfolio of varied enterprises. Erica Nicole is best known by the entrepreneurial community as the Founder of the internationally acclaimed and award-winning YFS Magazine: Young, Fabulous & Self-Employed (www.YFSentrepreneur.com). YFS Magazine is one of the largest independent small business news sites and a definitive digital resource for small business news and entrepreneurial culture.

Estelle Reyes
**Los Angeles Program
Director, Network For
Teaching
Entrepreneurship**

Dear Estelle,

At 16, I know that you are feeling on top of the world. You are probably getting ready for your high school graduation and are excited about college and the world beyond. Your loving family and supportive friends have guided you along the path thus far, but now it is your turn to create your own adventures. And trust me – your journey is going to be incredible!

At nearly double your age, I have some words of wisdom to light your path:

1.) **Follow Your Gut:** Your intuition is powerful and will always lead you to a better place. You are probably weighing many options in your head— anything from who are your real friends or what college to go to. Whenever you are faced with a tough decision, consult with those who you know and are most concerned about your well being (your parents, your teachers, your mentors). Pray about it and be open to hearing God's path for you. You know in your heart of hearts what is right for you so trust that when you make that decision, it's the right one.

2.) **Be Humble:** You will accomplish quite a bit in the next 15 years of your life and explore careers beyond what you currently envision. But always remember that you are only able to do this because of the love of your family, teachers and friends. Be grateful for your blessings and whenever possible give to others who may not necessarily have had all of the opportunities afforded to you. Be both inspired and inspiring.

3.) **Dream Big!:** I know you envision an extraordinary future for yourself. And I know that you have the capability of making those dreams a reality. Don't ever settle or sell yourself short. You have worked too hard to get to where you are not to pursue whatever it is that you want— studying abroad in Spain, getting a graduate degree learning how to DJ— and yes, you will do all those things! Continue to dream big and big things will come your way!

I am so proud of who you are at 16 and am excited about all of the things to come! Remember to always be yourself and be a positive role model to younger girls around you.

As a Motivational speaker and author Marianne Williamson shares:

> *"Our deepest fear is not that we are inadequate.*
> *Our deepest fear is that we are powerful beyond measure."*

Embrace that power and let your light shine!
Your future self (I promise, it only gets better!),

Estelle, 31

꿈ᄋ곰

Estelle Reyes joined NFTE in 2006 as Program Director and played a central role in launching and growing the NFTE Program in Los Angeles to reach 4,000 students locally. In 2010, Estelle was named Executive Director of NFTE Greater Los Angeles. In this role she manages staff, operations, fund development and major partnerships. She works in tandem with the NFTE National Executive Committee, the local Advisory Board and E-Council to chart the course of NFTE Los Angeles' quality and expansion. Estelle holds a Bachelor's degree from Brown University, and a Master's degree from the Harvard Graduate School of Education. Estelle is a Leadership LA Fellow (Class of 2010) and sits of the Board of U.S. Renewables Group.

꿈ᄋ곰

Deida Massey

Celebrity Makeup Artist +
Founder, Reel Beauty

Dear Deida:
I never thought I would reach
a place of security in knowing
a place of security in knowing
who I was then and now. At 16 years old, I never
thought I knew it all, but I wanted it all. I was ambitious,
talented and extremely independent. With the wisdom
and knowledge I have attained today, I understand the
true meaning of knowing who you are. Participating and
engaging in situations that compromised my worth was
detrimental to my life. I can say to you as a woman
today; love yourself first when it comes to young men.
Never settle for less and always consider the
consequences. There were times when I had the choice
to say "no." There were times when I should've said
"no." See, I didn't know what true love was. I thought if
I had sex with him, he would love and accept me more.

That was a painful lesson. If I knew that lesson would cost me a trip into the emergency room, with three different STDs and potentially interfere with the most precious gift a woman could give to this world - a child - I would have said "no." I thought dating an older man made me a grown woman. I experienced something that none of my friends had. I found love in the arms of a man 5 years older than I.

What he saw was a vulnerable, gullible young girl who knew nothing about love. I thought the gifts, shopping sprees, and out of town vacations were his way of showing me I was the one. I was ignorant to the true meaning of love. My mama had shared with me how to be sexually responsible, but I didn't practice that with him because he told me he loved me. When he denied what he'd done and never came to see me in the hospital, I felt lonely and used.

I hid my emotions from my friends, my mother and even myself. I brushed it off like I had a bad infection when what happened to me almost cost me my life.

That was one hard lesson to learn and I had to realize he never loved me and I never loved myself. Without careful thought, I gave my mind, body and soul too freely.

Your soul is precious and it takes healing to restore what was broken. They say wait until you are married to have sex, and today, I can honestly say it is worth the wait. I know who I am and whose I am by allowing God to show me my worth through His Word. Take your life one step at a time and allow God to order your steps in love. God has given a clear definition of love; apply it to your life and watch God's treasurers unfold one day at a time.

With love,
Deida

‿∾⧉☙

Prior to pursuing her dream of being a makeup artist in the beauty, fashion, and entertainment industry, Deida obtained a Master's of Jurisprudence from Loyola School of Law in Child and Family Law. Today Deida Massey is the Founder and Executive Director of Reel Beauty, Inc – an organization that assists at risk urban girls. To date along with a team of dedicated consultants, board members, RBI alumni and volunteers, Reel Beauty, Inc. has mentored upwards 500 girls. Their outreach in the community has impacted the lives of young girl's throughout the city of Chicago. As a result, they have landed partnerships with: Girl Scouts of Greater Chicago and Indiana, University of Chicago Project's Exploration, The Nellie Prather Foundation, E.L.F. Cosmetics, Gear-Up, Brand Jordan, The Clorox Foundation, Clear Channel Communications and Louis Vuitton to name a few.

‿∾⧉☙

Bridgette Wright
Producer

Dear Bridgette,

There are so many things I want to tell you. It may seem like every choice you make early in your life will be a difficult one because you grew up too fast and did too many adult things way before your time. Your dreams are deferred since the strain of having money and the lack of knowledge of how to go after what you want is a constant reminder that maybe your dream was just too big.

That's not true. Never give up on the desires of your heart. God put them there for a reason. The absence of your father's presence and the abuse that you saw in your mother's marriage all play a huge part in the woman you become. I would love to give you all the answers and be a shoulder for you to cry on when life gets rough or you feel you're not good enough. I want to be there to take the pill bottle out of your hand when you contemplate life being better on the other side after your heart gets broken. Today at 36 I have all of the answers, but what I will tell you is this: If you live your whole life being a victim of circumstances that were beyond your control, you won't have much of a life. You'll spend it in a mode of constant suffering.

You'll never be satisfied or truly happy, and you'll always be waiting for the ball to drop. Forgive the people that hurt you, and have enough faith in yourself to go after your dreams sooner than later. Your spiritual foundation will be your compass, so stay the course. Prayer is your best friend and will give you comfort when nothing else will. Know your worth, and stop selling yourself short every time a guy looks as if he loves you. You're so much better than that, and All of those things are real problems, and yes, all of those things have happened to you, but they don't define you. I won't sit here and say that even most of them are not good enough anyway. Don't fear the unknown. Embrace it. Life is a journey, and if you knew what was around every corner, there would be no point in even living it.

You are a very talented person with a smile that can light up a room. You have the whole world waiting for you to display those talents so fear is not an option. Strive to be successful, but don't lose yourself in it. Success can be tricky, and you can't live off of it alone so stay grounded. I want you to know that love can be a vulgar four letter word if given prematurely so love yourself first before you love a man. Be honest about what you want and what you need and what you can give.

Try not to live your life by the clock of society; that's a sure way to be unhappy so take your time and do what works for you. People aren't perfect, Bridgette, even when you want them to be so mistakes are inevitable. When someone tries to rectify a mistake, don't push them away. Forgiveness will be your most difficult lesson. Don't become a slave to your pain. Forgive those who didn't know better, and allow your heart to heal. Bridgette, I struggle with how I want to end this letter. I fear that maybe I haven't said enough but above all else, enjoy your life. Don't waste it being mad at the world or feeling like you got the short end of the stick because most people feel this way. It's what you do with the short end that makes you special. Now go get'em and never look back!

I love you,
Bridgette

Bridgette began as a freelance producer for the short film Beyond Essays, an American Sign
Language film and the award winning short film CHANGE, a film about the irony of Prop 8 passing during the 2008 election. CHANGE has screened at multiple festivals throughout the world and received a Honorable Mention at Athens International Film Festival and nominated for best short at Texas Black Film Festival. She attends the UCLA's producing program and is a member of Film Independent. She is also the Owner/CEO of S6xth
House Entertainment film production
company located in Los Angeles, CA.

Tracy Marlbrough
Social Worker + Founder, R.I.S.E. Up

Dear Tracy,

Being a woman takes strength, compassion, confidence, courage, style, grace and countless other adjectives to describe what a woman embodies. My journey as a woman has come with joy, laugher, sorrows, pains, setbacks and most of all, blood, sweat and tears. But through it all, God has kept me and supplied me with His grace and mercy. Rise up! Shake off the guilt, pain, rejection, depression, loneliness, despair, bitterness, low self esteem, or anything that has you bound and anything that or that hinders you from reaching your destiny.

A confident woman is able to respect herself and others, smile on contact, lead by example, and ignore rude looks and comments. A confident woman speaks with sincerity, smiles with warmth, hugs with love, and gives without expecting anything in return.

Strive to be a woman of noble character, style and grace. It's important that our beauty is not only outward; "but the hidden person of the heart, in the incorruptible adornment of a gentle and quiet spirit, which in the sight of God is very precious". (1 Peter 3:4) Do not doubt for a moment your worth; you are more precious than rubies, chosen by God, predestined for greatness, and powerful beyond measure. Allow your confidence to exude from your heart into the atmosphere. Once your confidence comes out, you will feel free to be you. Stand with your head lifted and chest out. Leave your imprint on the world. God has given you a gift and purpose; take root and grow. There will be obstacles but remember to stay anchored in the Lord, and trust His word. Allow him to guide your path into your journey as a woman.

Love,
Tracy Marlbrough

Tracy Marlborough is a young woman living Los Angeles, California where she was born and raised. A graduate of Crenshaw High school, who is set to acquire her bachelor's degree in Sociology from California State University-Northridge in 2011. Tracy is a member of Alpha Kappa Alpha Sorority Inc. wherein she continues to commit herself to several community service projects. In 2010, Tracy started her nonprofit organization- RISE UP Youth Empowerment Inc. The sole purpose of RISE UP Youth Empowerment Inc., is reaching at-risk teens and young women through faith based principles.

ഇന്റെ

Cari Kaufman
Author + Speaker + Life Coach

Dear Cari,

Not in a million years did I believe I would end where I am today. There were hundreds- no thousands - of tiny steps along the way that led me to this place and I am so, so grateful for them all. I have often said that while I wouldn't want anyone to trace my footsteps, I wouldn't change them either. My journey has been far too valuable in shaping the amazing, powerful and beautiful woman that we have become.

But if I am honest, that statement isn't entirely true. I would change many things for you. If I could save you some of the pain and heartache and loneliness and yet still impart to you the wisdom, compassion and strength that those experiences carried with them, I would do so. What a wonderful gift to be given the opportunity to transcend time and space and share just a little of that wisdom with you now.

Cari, the most precious and immeasurable gift that this arduous journey has given us is an unshakeable faith and knowledge of the Lord, Jesus Christ. (I see you rolling your eyes!) I know where you are in your faith journey- you feel so lost, alone and your soul is crying out for truth. If I could give you anything, right now that would radically change the course of our lives, it would be this Truth. How different would we be if we left off the never-ending, always alone, search for a love that only the God of the universe could provide? I cannot even fathom it.

The greatest lesson I have learned- one that I am still learning every day- is so simple, yet so hard for me to grasp. Never let any human being, including yourself, determine your worth. They will always underestimate your value. The only one who can truly measure your worth is God, and to him, you are "his treasure"- a prize so highly valued that he sacrificed his only begotten son just for the chance to reconcile you to him. No man, no friend, no human being, no other god can love you like that, and it is unfair to expect it.

Derive your value – your identity – only from the fact that you are the beloved daughter of the King of kings.

Cari, as you move through your life on this journey to womanhood, you will seek the love of a good man. Along the way, we've looked under rocks and in dark alleyways. We've accepted mediocre and sometimes cruel treatment of our tender heart in our search for that love. Let me just tell you this- we didn't find it in those places. We found it in a man who would take time out from his friends to teach us how to throw a football. We found it in a man who would keep watch while we slept to make sure we didn't miss a final. We found it in a man who would challenge us to push through tough times in our life and persevere even when it was difficult. We found love in a man who would never accept from us mediocrity, but who would never require from us perfection. Love was a saint in red Chucks. He was an unexpected but absolutely perfect choice.

Love will take you by surprise. She's not a mistress that plays hard to get. Wait for her, and you won't be sorry.

Cari, the last and final wisdom I would give you is one I am just learning.

You are not the message.

We've been uniquely gifted as a multi-faceted communicator. Words will be your tool to inspire, persuade, and touch the lives of people all over the world. God will gift you and equip you, but there is a battle ahead of you.

Whatever message you choose to bring, understand this: there is a difference between living your message and being the message. To live your message is to fully embrace it. It is to understand your calling and to understand what you are calling others to and to assimilate and incorporate it into your life. Living your message leaves room for error, for mistakes and for failure. When you live your message, a failure doesn't invalidate the message- it simply makes it human. We have spent a good deal of our life trying to be the message, and, let me tell you, no human being is capable of that. Being the message allows the inevitable mistake to invalidate it.

It allows the experience of rejection to cripple and wound it, and it opens the door for a lot of heartache and bitterness. As a messenger, you are simply responsible for wrapping the package and delivering the gift. It is not your responsibility to make sure it is received or opened. When someone rejects your message, they are not rejecting you.

Cari, you are a beautiful and strong young woman and you will grow to be an amazing mother, wife and friend. Whatever path you choose, relish the journey- both good and bad times. Learn from your experiences and approach each day as a gift to be opened. There is love and blessing in absolutely every ounce of life you experience. Embrace it all.

"Live each moment as an unrepeatable miracle. Which is exactly what it is: unrepeatable and a miracle."

Much love,
Cari Kaufman

Cari Kaufman graduated from the University of Arkansas and was commissioned as an officer in the United States Army and spent four years serving her country in one of the most highly deployed units in the American military. She was awarded the prestigious Soldier's Medal for Heroism, after rescuing a young girl from a gang rape and single handedly dispatching several attackers. After leaving the military, Cari became the factory manager in a plastics manufacturing facility. In May 2007, Cari left her position as a case manager with an eldercare agency to start her own successful coaching business, GPS 4life.net. Cari gave her life to Christ on September 19, 2002 after 10 years of practicing the occult. In 2009, Cari surrendered her life and business to God's call to full time women's ministry. She is dedicated to using her ability to bring groups and teams together to common ground to build up women's ministry groups across the country. Cari lives with her fabulous husband, Charlie in Northwest Arkansas and they have two amazing children, Alexander and Elizabeth.

Charisse Nesbit
**Development Executive,
Lions Gate Entertainment**

Dear Chari,

People have often described you as an "old soul," or just an old woman according to your not-so-subtle sister's assessment, and it's true. There is so much you already know right now that will not change with age. Wherever it came from, there is a lot of knowledge within you already that you must learn to accept and trust.

People will tell you a lot of things about who they think you are, but you know what is true so don't ever allow anyone to change what you already know about yourself. No one else has to walk in your shoes but you so trust that you wear them well and keep your step sure on the path you choose. You've had a challenging beginning to life, and as you grow, you will come to love a singer named Billie Holliday.

Though her journey was much rougher than any you will ever experience, there is a lot you will learn from her. The most important of which came in her song "God Bless The Child." Though your parents have not always been there for you and often will not be in the future, you have to realize that their actions don't define you or what you can do. Listen to Billie's words and know that despite what your parents do, you will be okay. You are blessed. You can make your own way and may be called upon to do so from time to time. While you will sometimes only have yourself to depend on, know that you do have people who are willing to help and allow them to do this from time to time. You don't always have to do it on your own, but know that you can if it is necessary. Don't be afraid to trust yourself and your instincts to get you through life's tough patches.

You have always been one to burn on the inside while appearing calm on the outside. While it's good to let it out, be careful of how you do it. You are often quick with your opinions but know that they are not for everyone, nor does everyone have the insight into your thoughts.

Words have power and can hurt so while you don't have to censor yourself, do be aware of how what you say can impact the way you are perceived. Often it can be misconstrued, but take responsibility for your part in this. Just because you feel that something is true, know that not everyone agrees with your truth, and it's okay to sometimes keep that to yourself. Whether you feel you are in the right or not, the wrong words can have a lasting effect. Sometimes it's okay to keep it to yourself and not share things that others may not be ready to hear. While your life will take many twists and turns, know that you already know what it is you want out of it. You are a free spirit with a strong will. No matter how much you attempt to deny who you are and what you want, you will only delay the inevitable because you are not good at denying yourself of what you want. Don't be afraid to go out and get what you want the first time! Time is promised to no one, so the sooner you do what makes you happy, the more time you will have to enjoy it. Also, you will find that often your first instinct is always right. Denying what you really want to do with your life only leads you down the wrong path before finally getting on the right one. Trust yourself enough to know that what you want is always the right path. Trying to stick to what is "sensible" is not an option that works for you as you are not one to continue with a lie. Start with the truth and stick with it. If you do second guess your instincts, know that you can always get back to where you need to be.

Every detour in life is just a new way into where you will end up. If it takes you longer to get there, so be it. Know that that there are no accidents in life, only new lessons to be learned. Always try to find the lessons and apply them. Don't ever regret the choices or mistakes you may make in your life because it will all come full circle.

You've seen it already, and you will continue to learn this as life goes on. Just as there are no new stories to be told, there are no problems that you can't overcome, find your way through, and eventually make work for you. Someone once told you that nothing comes from sleeping but a dream. While you are awake and listening, know that you have the power to make those dreams come true!

Love,
Charisse Nesbit

ℰℑℭℜ

Charisse Nesbit is a Director in the Production and Development Department at Lionsgate. A graduate of The University of New Mexico where she earned her Bachelor's Degree in Journalism, she received her Master of Fine Arts degree from Columbia College Chicago in Fiction Writing. Deciding to expand her horizons, she came to Los Angeles through the Columbia College Semester in L.A. Producing Program, eventually landing at Lionsgate where she worked her way up from intern, to consultant, to her current position. She is also the author of the novella, "Learning to Scream," had an essay featured in "Children of the Dream: Our Own Stories of Growing up Black in America, and was editor and contributor to the book "A Dream Deferred A Joy Achieved: Foster Care Stories of Survival and Triumph" which was published by Strebor Books, an imprint of Simon and Schuster. She is happy to be involved in bringing the Obie Award winning play "For Colored Girls Who Have Considered Suicide When the Rainbow is Enuf" to the screen as a Co-producer and is also working on two projects with Harpo Films, one of which will star Chris Rock.

Tatiana Jerome
Fashion Entrepreneur

Tatiana,

I know you have never been common nor have your interests been ones that fit in, but what you may not know is that your sense of self is valuable. You may wonder how it is that you went from fitting in to standing out. This really isn't that hard to answer as you have never fit in. While you have been taught to follow a path that is sure to guarantee you a less stressful future, you are a natural born path creator. I know you shake when told what to do. I know you get bored with a predictable path so you make your own rules. You set your own traditions. I'm telling you to break away from the thoughts of constant human protection and instant approval because your truth will be challenged. While you feed yourself into self vanities and express your need for challenge through your everyday designs in the arts, the world has another plan for you.

53

The world is asking you for your sacrifice. The world is asking you to forget what made you laugh and what gave you peace and move in a uniform direction with other people. You think because you avoided alcohol, sex, smoking and so forth, you have a future, but the truth is that once you have sacrificed yourself to this earth, you have killed the most important part of your very existence: your truth. You have loved God from the beginning and walked with Him as He has always nurtured and loved you. He stood as your truth and had a value that no one could afford. Yet with time, the world has found a way to get you to sell your truth for what you believed was rare gold, only to be tricked into getting fool's gold. Forget the opinions of others as they dissipate your own thoughts. Walk past the judgment of those that 'once were' as they have created a maze to which they cannot find the beginning. You must love, adore, value, honor and preserve the language of truth.

You will find that what you leave behind is more important than what you came with. Act with good intentions. Know that your first instinct is one that arises from love and protection, so acknowledge it.

Rise above reckless chatter. You will never be satisfied with simplistic surface pleasures. You force yourself to enjoy the temporary when you know that your very existence feeds off of meaning. You move in a direction in which you believe there is more for your mind. You are a Queen that has already brought attention to yourself. Do not back away from it. Stay in tune with your foundation. As time goes by and life may not seem to be what you expected, do not be disappointed as it is only up to you to change what you choose to see. You love a challenge so sticking to your life's desires will be your biggest one. So many distractions will come your way, and you will entertain them. I'm telling you now to commit yourself to you. You were not brought up to entertain or play "the game" of life. You exist because you have a passionate Father who knows that you are destined to be an influencer. Don't worry about time; just keep moving, exploring and rebelling from injustice. Conforming to the norm has no meaning or place within you. You're still young; do not ever give up on yourself.
*P.S. Don't give the world what they can handle, give the world what they will never be ready for.
From a Love that grew up,
Tatiana Jerome

ശ‌ൿ

Growing up, Tatiana was always fascinated in the arts and spent her time exploring the many facets of her creativity. She designed several pieces of her own clothing as well as assisted her others in coordinating the right looks. In whatever she put her name on, her heart was attached to it. She graduated from Florida A & M University with a Bachelors in Science in Public Relations. Upon graduation, Tatiana went right to work in starting her first business, Pink Cherie. Pink Cherie caters to the woman who knew herself. As discriminating as Tatiana was to fashion, she understand other women were as well and continued to pursue her love. While growing Pink Cherie, she started P. Series Stylist which assist women in establishing trademark looks. Later on came I'm Faith Fitted, which provides support to others who are in need of a support system in going after their dreams. Tatiana enjoys meeting and communicating with people from all over. With a compassionate heart, she places her successes on her strong relationship with God and strong support team of family and friends. While already being covered by magazine and other press, Tatiana finds solitude and complete accolade in giving.

Cheryl Isaac
Entrepreneur + Writer

Dear Cheryl,
You're a young lady now :-) It's amazing—the journey you've taken to get here. When I think of everything you've surpassed in order to be where you are, my eyes well up with tears of gratefulness to the infinite power that has kept you. I'm writing this letter as a plea, but please don't think that I'm attempting to patronize your teenage wisdom.

I understand that your sixteen-year old eyes have weathered the storm of a sixty-year olds. In just a few years, you've witnessed the disastrous result of misplaced power in Liberia, the countless consequences of greed, and what the feelings of ineptitude can do to people. You said this yourself. I read this in stunned amazement as I read through your journals. I guess I never imagined that you would be writing such perceptive analysis at your age. It's taken me years to fully grasp the picture—at sixteen, you've already lived through the war scenes of a Danielle Steel novel, and you probably loved reading *The Diary of Anne Frank* so much because at times you've felt as if you know her. Cheryl, I want you to feel safe. I'm writing to ask you to trust in life again. Although you may think that love is a four-letter word banned from your vocabulary, that life is about survival and not fulfillment, and that true relationships are a myth, I want to assure you that years will prove your theories wrong. I know you feel out of place now that you're here in America—you can't even eat in the lunch room without some kid asking you whether you had a tail and lived in trees in Africa—but everything will be better within a few years. I want you to grow older to embrace these experiences so that other young women feel safe to harness theirs. This may sound cliché but try to focus on your education and your goals for now. Do what you can to drown the nightmares of your past, so that you focus on who you can become. I understand that you're young and want to be hip, but don't obsess about fitting in. The thing is, you never did fit in. You were always a little different—awkwardly shy with a circumspect curiosity—and that's OK! Your true friends will accept you and not judge you. Remember the boy who started to have a crush on you after he saw you give your 9th grade valedictorian speech in Liberia?

See? Nerds still have some fun ;-) Think about that, and forget about the popular kids who never invite you to their parties, or the ones who make up mean jokes about you.

I wanted this letter to reach you before you give up on being all that you can be, and before you drown yourself in self pity because you continue to wish you had the childhood of the ones who mock you. Please let these thoughts warm your heart as you morph into the adult woman that you will become: you may not have had much of a childhood but you have a child story. You're not strange, you're just *different*. Don't let your past defeat you, instead, let it *empower* you. You may not understand this now, but please believe me when I say that you will understand it later.

Sincerely,
Cheryl

Cheryl Isaac is an entrepreneur and writer. Cheryl works with small businesses and entrepreneurs on strategic business planning and growth. She lives in Ohio with her family.

Wadooah Wali
Producer + Communications Executive

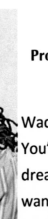

Wadooah,
You're hungry. You have big dreams. The first thing I wanna tell you is to always remember to breathe. Breathe deep and enjoy that moment that the breath is drawn into your body. Enjoy the quiet calm that accompanies each and every breath and know that special time/space perspective that you've created for yourself is yours and yours alone. I know that you do this already. Keep it up! One of our strengths things that keeps you moving, keeps you able to focus on what's important vs. not, what allows you to rationalize and see the forest for the trees, keep your head while all others around you have lost it is your ability to pause, breathe, rationalize and then act. Practice makes perfect and you're already off to an amazing start. Keep it up as it will continue to serve you/us well.

Okey doke. All breathing exercises aside, I really wanted to share with you what will be one of our greatest personal achievements to date that was the result of a big dream...Our first documentary film. This film is significant for many reasons, but particularly, it's significant in both in terms of the subject matter, but also because it is the symbolic embodiment of pursuing a life-long dream of wanting to tell a story that we wanted to tell...Your story, our story.

It is a story that we dreamed up and brought to life using the visual medium of documentary film for telling a story that will hopefully inspire, ignite and unite audiences. No matter what happens, at the end of the day, we did it, proving to ourselves, our parents and yes, even the world, that once again, "Yes. We can." The hunger, the drive, the desire to succeed at all costs serving as the fuel that fed the motivation to show that I can do anything that I set my mind to, no matter what the circumstance, the obstacles that present themselves in my path, the unfathomable fear factor, the nagging voices of negativity and self-doubt. Against all odds, we did it...I did it...you, will do it.

Well-meaning parents, grounded in reality, growing up in and living through the school of hard knocks, who over-came the racism of their time and instilled that same sense of pride in their five kids, only to still be constrained by the reality of life. Their reality hinging on survival and making it through each day, one day at a time precluded them from dreaming big. Thank goodness, they encouraged dreaming. Only, for them dreaming was one thing, living was another and dreaming too big was unrealistic without that tangible something that could link a cold reality to a big dream. Unless they could see it, it couldn't be achieved. You listened a little and accepted this programming somewhat when they told you to "find a new profession" when you told them years before age 16 that you wanted to be a writer, director, producer and make films. Their well-meaning advice at the time was backed up by their assertion that there were no successful, black, female writer-director-producers in Hollywood. Their fear that we would become a "starving artist" they passed along as their evidence that it couldn't be done. In the years before age 16, there was no disputing the parents and there was no denying the wisdom of their years. No denying, but we never let it go...

Teenage love we never had/experienced. We were still trying to get through the challenges of life, which at age 16 now include divorced parents and baby-crack-head-daddy drama. This means getting through high school, keeping the grades up, showing up for school activities, taking on leadership positions, thinking about and planning for college and then going home, cooking, cleaning, doing homework, making sure the siblings did their homework, settling sibling rivalries and making sure the house was at some state of normalcy by the time mom walked through the door. Who am I through all of this? Strip down the band-and-other high-school-activity-loving, intelligent, well-spoken, honor student, who's also an older sister to three others, younger sister to an older brother all of whom have Arabic names and who were raised Muslims in the South. Strip it down further. Am I gay? Am I straight? Do I like boys? Do I like and trust people? I don't look like other people. I don't talk like other people. Other people don't talk like me. Do they like me? Am I pretty? What is pretty? Do I wanna be pretty? In comparison to some, I'm a big teenage girl.

. I hate shopping. My mom can rarely afford to take me to the mall or department stores to go shopping, but she does when she can. Only, we never see eye-to-eye on what I should wear. I have drag queen size feet and she takes me to the "Women's" department for older lady clothes, both because the clothes there fit my body shape better and because she doesn't want me in anything that will draw in unwanted male attention that could lead to sex and/or any other type of inappropriate behavior for a young lady.

Oh yeah, I am a young woman, but don't even think about painting my nails or putting on make-up, though I'd kind of like to experiment with that stuff, even if only for a minute. Just to shake the Muslim girl stigma that has enshrouded us our entire childhood and be "normal." Like the other young women my age. I'd also like to talk about my fake teenage boy crush...that's what everyone talks about. If only I had "cool" clothes or even "cool" shoes. A "cool" backpack. I try carrying a purse, but I keep leaving the danged thing behind and it gets stolen every time.

On some levels, I know that this just isn't for me. I know that it doesn't feel right and on many levels, I know that once I leave the backdrop of Eastside High School in Gainesville, Florida, that many of these worldly things don't matter. Keep that in your brain and never let it go. We knew at 16 what we know now...that there's a whole big world out there and what matters most is to live it in the best possible way, whatever that is, as long as it makes you happy. Dream big beyond your current state of awkward, unknown yuck to something else. Something different and away, always, hoping for something better.

Somewhere in there, you know that you just have to be you. That's what it means on a day-to-day basis. It's in there now. Kicking around...You know there's nothing wrong with you. I'm here to tell you to stay with that thought. Grow it. Own it. Now, at age 37, people gravitate toward you. They did then at age 16, so, GOOD NEWS! This is an on-going thread. Somehow, somewhere, the beautiful you came out to play. Maybe it was there at age 16, maybe it was before then. Regardless, you made a film loosely about our struggle to tune out the backdrop of noise that tried to tell us that we weren't good enough because of various factors and that didn't encourage us to be our best selves in our current form. We made a film that tries to help people (myself included) understand and continually keep the notion that beauty is in the eye of the beholder and that there is beauty in everything so we should erase the self -hate and the self doubt and just love and appreciate who we are. And once we're able to shed the pounds, the societal weight and weight of self, then we not only are we able to love ourselves, but we're able to love and appreciate others and once we're able to do that, we can love and appreciate the world around us. Grandiose mission this film, this dreaming big. But that's who we are and what we do. It's what makes life interesting and exciting from day-to-day and week-to-week. What a difference a day makes. In spite of a longer path and slight detour through corporate America, in which we've also done well and rocked the boat, we stayed true to a dream and a desire to tell a story. Is it the best story we've ever told? No. Will it be the last one?

I sincerely doubt it and hope not. Being a good corporate story-teller is a well-honed skill that will only complement and enhance our creative story-telling and currently I still plan to have my cake and eat it too in that department. We know age 16-37, that life is not an either/or proposition. Life is what happens when you live it and that's what we are here on this earth to do. If we can do it, be happy and make the world a better place in the process, then that's what we live to do. What a difference many weeks over many years make. At age 37, I'm still going because you at age 16 willed it. Thank you for propelling me forward. If nothing else, I hope that the idea of your 37-year-old me will continue to push us to new, untold, yet-to-be-dreamed heights. For now, let's get back to us and do what makes you come alive, for that's what the world needs (so the saying goes), but more importantly, that's what you need. Now. Take in some air and just breathe.

Deepest Love,
-w2
Wadooah Wali

Wadooah Wali is a communications specialist with more than 15 years of diverse experience who blends her passion for communications, social media and technology with creativity. Wadooah joined Demand Media as one of the two original founding communications team members in 2006. Currently, as Senior Director of Corporate Communications, she manages internal and external communications and has since lead the many of the company's communications activities and Demand Media's sites like eHow, typeF.com and Cracked.com. In addition to other business initiatives, she worked closely with the executive team in taking the company public in January 2011 - the largest internet/tech IPO since Google's in 2004. Wadooah earned a Bachelor of Arts degree in Mass Communications from the University of South Florida.

Charlotte Ponticelli

Senior Coordinator,
International Women's Issues,
U.S. State Department

Dear Charlie,

It has been a long time but I still think of you a lot. If I were to describe you to my friends, what would I say? Maybe this: That you are really into rock-and-roll (especially the Beatles); you love books and use them to escape from the everyday world; you work hard in school and though you're often cutting up in class and end up getting detention, you usually get good grades (except in math, which you hate!). You often feel very awkward and insecure and yet you dream about all the different things you'd like to do when you grow up, just like some of the heroines in your books – Florence Nightingale, Joan of Arc, Nancy Drew.

I know that as one of six children in your family, you're close to your brothers and sisters but you sometimes feel like the odd one out, since your two older brothers always like to make fun of you and your mother's always reminding you that as the oldest girl, you're the one who has to look after the younger ones and set a good example.

It's your mother who keeps you "down to earth" (the value of common sense!), but it's your father who encourages your dreams. He tells you that as long as you work hard, there's no limit to what you can do. You hold onto his words and think about them all the time. And you love both of your parents for what each of them has taught you, especially when it comes to faith in God, putting family first, service to others and reaching, always reaching for the stars.

You would tell me that all of this is being put to the test right now as you approach your 16th birthday. Your family has just moved to another state – in the middle of the school year! – and you're now the "new kid" in a smaller school where the girl who's the class bully likes to call you some pretty mean names. Now more than ever you try to escape through books and movies, but you also volunteer at the local hospital and try to take your mind off your own troubles by helping others. You're working harder than ever at your studies and start to think about college. You're finding out you have a talent for languages, and Spanish is your favorite subject. You dream about distant countries and what it would be like to see the world!

So let me tell you now, four decades later, what the future holds for you, dear fifteen-year-old Charlie. After a lot of hard work, you will get scholarships and go to college, where you will major in Spanish. You will spend two years studying in Spain and complete your Master's degree. You will fall in love with a man who encourages your dreams, and you will discover the world of public service – working in the U.S. Senate, the White House, and the U.S. Department of State. You will meet Presidents and heroic people leading the cause for f reedom and opportunity in many distant countries. You will see the world! You will have children – two wonderful sons – and your brothers and sisters are still your best friends. You still think of your parents every day, and you grow closer and closer to your faith, knowing that "God plants you where he needs you." You will dedicate yourself to many different service projects at church and within your community, but you will never forget how important it is just to laugh and to try to bring joy to this often difficult, mixed-up world. Enjoy the journey! Never lose heart! God bless!

Love,
Charlie

ဆၢ

Charlotte M. (Charlie) Ponticelli is an international and
government affairs expert with extensive experience in
Washington, D.C. She began her career on Capitol Hill and served
most recently as Deputy Under Secretary for International Labor
Affairs at the U.S. Department of Labor. Previously, Mrs. Ponticelli
served as the State Department's Senior Coordinator for
International Women's Issues; Senior Advisor for State's Bureau of
Population, Refugees, and Migration; Director of Human Rights in
State's Bureau for International Organization Affairs; Congressional
Liaison for Latin America and the Caribbean at the U.S. Agency for
International Development; and Director of Congressional
Correspondence in the Legislative Affairs Office of the White
House. In the private sector, Mrs. Ponticelli has been Program
Director for the Balkans within the Eastern European Division of
the International Republican Institute, Director of Media Relations
at the Becket Fund for Religious Liberty; and Director of Lectures
and Seminars at the Heritage Foundation in Washington, D.C. Mrs.
Ponticelli is the recipient of several Superior Honor Awards from
the Department of State and USAID, the Veritas Award from
Albertus Magnus College, and the Outstanding Young Alumna
Award from her alma mater, Hood College in Frederick, Maryland.
Most recently, she received the Loyalty Award from the American
Women for International Understanding, the Inspiration Award
from the Foreign Investment Network and Global Trusted Alliances
and the "Afghan-American Sisterhood Award" from Ariana
Outreach. Mrs. Ponticelli received her Bachelor of Arts
degree in Spanish literature from Hood College and her
Master of Arts degree through New York University's
program in Madrid. She also completed two years of
doctoral studies in Spanish at The Catholic University of America
in Washington, D.C.

Sherrell Dorsey
Natural Beauty Expert

Dear Sherrell,

I know you are in one of the most awkward stages in your life right now. On top of striving to be an overachiever, you are on a journey to discovering your identity. And that's okay. But we have to deal with the reality of the tough things you are going through. Don't hold it inside anymore. It's okay to be verbal about your feelings. Strength isn't always about taking and enduring the pain; sometimes it means releasing the pain in order to heal. Put your pain, anger and frustration aside. It will get better... I promise. Running away from your problems won't change them nor will they disappear. You want to leave home for college not just to pursue great things, but to leave the past behind. I get that, but at some point you will need to go home to restore yourself or the burden will follow you.

It's okay to be in this state right now, but know that you need to call on God. He will be faithful to you. He will be your identity while you search for what that means to you. Give Him your troubles and your frustrations. Trade them in for peace, love and joy. Your anger will only get in the way and hold you back from being the woman He is calling you to be. Know yourself. Don't continue to look for love and acceptance in the wrong places. Yes, growing up in a single-parent household isn't easy.

Dealing with loss and dysfunction in your family does not make you designed or destined for destruction. You get to decide how you respond. Rise above it, and know that you are worthy of more. You were designed for more. You are worthy to be loved. Protect yourself, your body, your mind and your spirit. Don't let anyone that isn't worthy take you for granted. I know you walk around with this void you want to fill. But only God can do that. No person, relationship or material item can clothe emptiness, baby girl. Let love fill that void. Let peace fill that void. You will survive a lot of heartbreak, confusion and self-destruction if you just believe. If you just forgive. If you just stand still and listen. Your life, how you come into this world, does not define your destiny.

God already decided for you. He created you to have abundance. Don't settle, Sherrell. This isn't the end. Remember that Jesus was born in a barn with no doctors, no balloons and no wealth. He was born in a barn amongst smelly animals and manure. But that didn't keep Him from fulfilling his purpose. You are loved. You are beautiful. Let your life show beauty to the world. Inspire and uplift others. Forgive so that you can heal. Don't carry around the burden anymore, Sherrell. Give it to God so that He can push you forward.

Love and Beauty,
Sherrell at 23

A passion for health, beauty, and fashion drove Sherrell Dorsey to educate herself in all areas and she made it her personal mission to inform her community about the dangers of living a toxic lifestyle while offering solutions on how to become healthier. After completing her degree in International Trade and Marketing for the Fashion Industries at the *Fashion Institute of Technology* in New York City, Sherrell yearned to learn more about skin care and cosmetics. She enrolled at the prestigious *Aveda Institute* to receive her aesthetics license. Fulfilling her dreams, Sherrell continues to educate women around the world through her workshops, articles and projects that help them to achieve beauty and wellness through positive guidance and holistic remedies. With entrepreneurship being a main focus, Sherrell continues to write for popular blogs and magazines and is currently working on her book and the opening of her own beauty store that will continue to teach others to Live Beautiful.

Cheryl Pullins

Life coach + Author

Dear Cheryl,

There are an abundance of things I wish someone had taken the time to tell me, in letter form or otherwise. Now, don't get me wrong, I was taught many valuable lessons while going through my teen years, many of which I continue to live by. One of the funniest lessons my mom taught me wasn't funny to me back then, but I find it humorous now. She would say, "Cheryl, don't go outside with rollers and a scarf on your head." As a teenage girl in the 1970's, I thought "how inconvenient." You see, during this time it was quite common to wear rollers and a head scarf until you were ready to get dressed up and head out to wherever you were going. But if you were just going to the corner store it was no big deal to go with rollers and a head scarf. Not in my house. It just wasn't allowed.

I shared that story because little did I know, that one lesson instilled in me the foundation for developing a positive self-image. I know what you are possibly thinking, "Self image? There is nothing wrong with my self-image." 'I look good." "I know how to dress." "I have lots of friends." "My friends are always commenting on my social media profiles and saying how good I look."

My dear, a solid self-image is rooted in more than outward appearance - hair, clothes, shoes, accessories or even friends. Self-image is the thing on the inside of you that says, "I am valuable." "I accept and celebrate my own uniqueness." "I am gifted and talented." "I am fearfully and wonderfully made."

The development of your self-image is watered and fertilized by powerful positive words that you think, hear, speak and believe about yourself. Over and over, day after day listen to, read, speak and believe positive words and phrases about you and your life. You may be thinking, "She must be kidding. I am not going to talk to myself. That doesn't make sense." Remember the story I shared with you earlier about no rollers and head scarves outside?

At the time, that didn't make sense to me either. Honestly, it was annoying. Anytime anyone was "telling me what to do." I was annoyed, but I still had to follow the rules. Little did I know that this one principle was going to help shape my self-image.

What I am sharing with you isn't about rules and regulations. I am sharing what is known as a guiding principle. No, not like the school principal. A guiding principle is something which you live by; it's a value, a code, or a foundational way of living. Growing a positive self-image requires you to adopt a way of getting rid of negativity, from your thoughts, words and environment and replacing it with positive, affirming words which will not only help to build your self-image but also change your life. Spend a few minutes every day speaking to yourself in positive and proactive terms. Here's a special bonus because you are indeed a special young lady. At the end of this letter, there are some positive phrases for you to speak to yourself every day. Have fun with it. Stand in front of a mirror and speak boldly to yourself. Don't be concerned about it feeling silly. You will be making a great impact on your life.

Well my dear, I am overjoyed that you have taken the time to read this heartfelt letter. I only desire the best for you because you deserve the best. You were created for such an incredible purpose and the earth awaits the arrival of the greatness within you. You are on your way. When you think you need a boost or some encouragement, just pull out this letter and read it. Know that you have some people cheering and rooting for you always. Repeat your positive phrases. Look in the mirror and say, "Yep, I am uber cool!"

Here are some positive phrases:

I am fearfully and wonderfully made.
I am beautiful on both the inside and the outside.
I was created to live a purposeful life.
I am valuable.
I love myself.
I embrace my unique ways.
I can do whatever I set my mind to do.
I live by the principles of honesty and integrity.

Lovingly yours,
Cheryl A. Pullins

8OC8

With passion, Cheryl is taking the message of victory to the world by sharing strategies and solutions for winning in business and life. Equipped as a certified life coach, Cheryl learned how to develop relationships and impart wisdom during her 20 year Human Resources profession. For over a decade she worked as part of the executive staff of the first and largest urban research park and also at an international multibillion dollar company. She developed and sharpened her leadership and training skills by working with C-level executives and ministries in the areas of leadership, administration and training. Cheryl is a multi-talented professional and motivational leader who leverages creativity and technology to deliver practical principles and solutions. She moonlights as a publisher, ministry consultant and radio show host. She is a contributing writer for both an award winning inspirational website and Rejoice Magazine. She has appeared on radio, TV and featured in several magazines. Cheryl is a Work Balance National Expert Advisor and Premier Coach for the National Association of Women on the Rise. Cheryl lives in Florida with her husband Zach, a specialized techie analyst. Date night is the highlight of her week and they both are computer junkies. She is a mom and grandmother of girls, girls, girls.

8OC8

Shonika Proctor

International Business Consultant

Hey there,
Little Miss Shonika,
I am here to tell you that it's good to wonder because it means you are alive an interacting and creating with and in the world. Life is good. YOUR LIFE IS GOOD. Your life is for good, and there is certainly nothing bad that can come from that. Absolutely nothing 'bad' can come from that. Wondering simply means you have a natural unfulfilled curiosity about things.

Curiosity leads to exploration. Exploration leads to discovery. Discovery leads to experimenting. Experimenting leads to learning. Learning leads to growth. Growth leads to accomplishments. Accomplishments lead to happiness. Happiness leads to satisfaction. Satisfaction leads to boredom. Boredom leads to wondering. And then you get to do it all again. You have to remember this because life is so dynamic and perpetually in motion.

You just have to know that at the end of the day, you are always moving forward even if it does not always seem that way. Remember the race between the turtle and the hare? The turtle won the race. Slow and steady wins the race time and time again.

On this day you may wonder if and how you will reach a big goal. And one day you will know with confidence that you will reach every goal that you really want. But you will mostly think about who can help you reach it, not how you will get there.

On this day you may be teased and called weird or different. And one day you will be called different and told how your individuality and creativity inspires others who wish they would have been that way when they were younger. On this day you may think about your career choices and how you will make a difference in the world. And one day you will be an entrepreneur (even though you may not know what that is yet) and make a difference in your every waking moment.

On this day you may not like school that much because it seems boring or you don't like being there because of 'certain things or people', but you will do the work anyway to just get through it. And one day you will realize that school was your business office that your parents' tax dollars paid for, your peers were your potential clients, and your teachers were your first consultants.

On this day you may wonder why people are so rude and mean. And one day you will realize that people often show love the way they are shown love. On this day you may wonder if you are making the right decision. And one day you will realize there are no wrong decisions. Every decision is right for you at the time you make it, even if it seems ethically or morally wrong. On this day you may wonder what others think about you. And one day you will realize that nobody thinks about you or remembers you unless you made them feel really special (for the good or the not so good). And during their life on this earth, they will always remember you that way unless your paths cross again and influences them otherwise.

On this day you may wonder if you'll ever have a boyfriend or significant other. And one day you will be very happy that you stayed focus on making money first, not making babies. Yes, you will meet a special person when you are not looking for him, and he will be far more beautiful, smarter and successful than the person of your dreams.

On this day you may wonder if one day you will be rich and famous. And one day you will realize the importance of saving and being smart with your money. You will build little by little and realize why not buying stuff you didn't really need was a good choice, a very good choice. On this day you may wonder if you will ever be popular. And one day you will realize that after your high school years, it doesn't matter anymore.

On this day you may wonder what you will be when you grow up. And one day you will realize life is more fun when you don't grow up because grown-ups always ruin the fun things! Seriously, you will choose a job that seems interesting to you, and it might seem like a very simple job at first.

But you will love that job and work very hard every single day as if one day you will be running the company...because you will! On this day you may wish you were more like those girls or those people. And one day you will learn that they always wished they were more like you. On this day you may be mad because you don't have a [fill in the blank]. And one day you will be so happy for what you received in its place.

On this day you may have a troubled relationship with your family or living circumstances. And one day you will appreciate the ability it gave you to relate and interact with so many different kinds of people with so many backgrounds. On this day you might complain about a lot of stuff that frustrates you. And one day you will make a bigger impact for causes you feel strongly about! On this day you will read books and look at a map and say one day I want to visit that place or that country on the other side of the world.
And one day you will go there and do a lot more than sightseeing and vacation! On this day you might wonder where you fit in. And one day you will be so glad that you didn't fit in...not even a little bit!

But I don't have to tell you this Shonika. You already know this. You know you are cool, even if no one else agrees. You know the unmet potential and possibilities that greets you each day. You know that at any moment, on any day, you can receive news that will change your life. It could be happy or sad news, but either way you will do amazing things after you choose to fully receive it and let it pass through you. Shonika, I truly love you as you are and would not change one single thing about you. In fact, I encourage you to keep on keeping on.

Keep writing. Keep creating. Keep volunteering. Keep observing. Keep dreaming. Keep socializing. Keep laughing. Keep playing. Keep learning. Keep saying thank you. Keep loving. Keep living fearlessly. Keep asking. Keep trying. Keep sharing. Keep being unreasonable. Keep being curious. Keep thinking. Keep looking for patterns and connections. I know it doesn't always make sense but just keep going. I know that others say don't look back. But I say do look back as you always have done. There are people, places and things that you have seen along your journey. They all have a purpose in your life. All the ideas and dreams you have thought of will never fade away.

They will come back stronger in their time as you are more capable of handling them.

On this day, in this very moment Shonika, you might still be wondering just what it all means.

And one day you'll just wonder.

And that will be perfectly fine....

....because wondering is life.

And life is good.

And YOUR LIFE is for good.

Sincerely,
Shonika

Shonika Proctor is a Washington, DC native currently living in Chile, South America. She has led a full and happy life having done everything from doing a National TV Commentary on the #1 Business TV Show in the U.S. (PBS Nightly Business Report) to traveling to see the real Santa Claus in Rovaniemi (Lapland), Finland. Shonika loves, loves, loves making cool and random things with cool and random people. She has created a lot of incredible things in the name of entrepreneurship and innovation with her rockstar teen innovators and change makers from all around the world. When Shonika grows up she wants to be a Toy Designer and Interactive Game Inventor (which she discovered a month shy of her 39th birthday). And then she will use all her money to build a modern day orphanage in the most beautiful and unbelievable place on Earth. But for now, Developing Chile into a first world nation keeps her pretty darn busy (and yes, her internal compass and a divine mystery led her there).

Christina Dunbar

Life Coach

My dearest younger Christina,

Settle in, get cozy, and allow this letter to offer you some peace. As a woman, you have so much power and strength, and the easiest way to connect with it is through joy. How do you find joy? Listen to your Soul. Your Soul is speaking to you all the time; you just need to get quiet and listen. No one else can guide you to greater joy and happiness. Trust your inner voice, listen to Her, act on Her desires. Trust yourself! Stop trying to be like anyone else. You are most magnetic, most radiant, and most appealing as you are-- funky and unique and different.

I want to save you years of trouble by adding this: stop thinking so much. You like to plan and figure things out, and all the while you wonder, "What is the best way?" You're always thinking! Life flows so much better when you just let go. Stop thinking and start feeling your way through it.

Don't force things to happen, just follow your passion, act on it in bold ways, and then surrender to the outcome. Follow your bliss, follow your heart, follow your pleasures.

I know you have a lot on your mind, so I made a little list you can glance at whenever you need to...

Boys, men, and love. Love comes to you when you are already in love-- in love with your life that is. Create a life full of the things you adore: good friends, dancing, journaling, hiking, giggling...you get the picture. Love your life first. And when you do attract your partner, here's a little secret: you actually change a man's behavior by the way you behave. Men, children, and even pets model their ways after women. It is the woman who sets the tone. We set the rules, the boundaries, and the guidelines. So know what you want and communicate it verbally. Be clear and speak up. The biggest mistake is thinking anyone can read your mind-- they can't.

Loss. I want you to know that every crisis, hard as it may be, is a sign from the Universe that things are shifting and changing so that you can grow. When things break down, shatter, and disappear, that means the "old you" is no longer being served by the situation and the "new you" is ready to emerge. Don't be afraid as life changes and shifts. There are cycles that come and go, and just as the seasons change, so will life. When it feels hard, express your frustration-- dance it out, write about it, take a kickboxing class, cry, sing, run. Just do me a favor and let your emotions out. Even though sadness and loss feels hard, it too is part of the journey. Express every emotion.

Confidence. You can build your confidence really quickly. Here's how: face your fears. Don't think about it; just do it. Your fears feel scary because they hold a lot of energy, and energy is powerful stuff. When you fear something-- face it, bust it open, and all the gold will spill out. Act confidently and soon you will feel confident.

Confusion. There is no right or wrong way. Life is full of twists and turns. When you feel confused, stop. Don't take action. Get quiet, go within, and get clear. What do you want? Forget about everyone else. What feels right to you? What feels good to you? You will never feel guilty or bad when you follow your Truth. Listen to your body, your Spirit, your Soul, your intuition, and you cannot go wrong.

With love,
Christina Dunbar

Christina Deena Dunbar is a Transformational Coach, Sensuality Specialist, speaker, author, and performer. She is creator and host of The Power and Pleasure tele-series, Branch Leader of The Goddess Collective- LA (an empowerment group for conscious women in business) and she is CEO of The Power Goddess. Christina's mission is to heal the blanket of shame that separates women from their Light. She does this by helping her clients ditch the Good Girl should's, **honor their sensual and Spiritual self**, **claim their voice, step into smokin' hot confidence, and create a fabulous future they're in love with.** Christina lives in sunny California with the love of her life; husband, friend, and partner, Chaim Dunbar.

Shavonna Cole

Teen Mentor

Dear Shavonna,
First, I know you are an introvert and like to keep to yourself more often than not. Life is not only about making ourselves happy and accomplishing goals. Life is also about relationships. I'm not just talking about dating. I'm talking about meeting people and getting to know others. Life is about building relationships with people; don't be so quick to cut people off. Don't be afraid to share your experiences, and make yourself willing to hear from others. You can learn so much from other people, and you may also have information that someone else may need. What I've come to learn is that everything you want to accomplish in life involves other people. As much as you may want to say that you don't need anyone to do what you want to do – you're wrong. You will need the hand or help from someone else, or some other company, organization, or business.

94

So as you travel through life's journey, pick up some friends along the way. Share a piece of you. Let others see what you have to offer the world; you never know what may come of it. Join some new clubs or groups, be part of a team, keep your employer's information, keep in touch with co-workers, and stay connected with people. This is what the adult world calls "networking". I have come to find out that it's the key to the world and fun to do, I might add. Don't be afraid of people; they may be just like you, or even better – they may be just the opposite!

Now let's talk about this college endeavor you're about to experience next year. There will be so many new experiences: new people, new places, new clubs, new classes, no parents, no adults checking on you all day, every day. College life is a whole new world, literally. It can be a great experience; it will be a great experience. But before you go, I want you to do this: Take out a sheet of paper, and write down the things or people or ideas that you value.

Place them in order of importance, and write down next to each item why you value that thing. After you finish, I want you to take that with you to college and put it somewhere you can always reference it. There are going to be situations that will challenge your beliefs and values, and it's very important that you stay true to them. You will have decisions to make, and there may be a time when you feel conflicted as to what decision to make – reference your paper. If you don't respect your values – others won't either! Don't be afraid to make your values known and stick to them. Trust me; you're going to need this one.

Next let's discuss "having relations". I know you're a virgin and right now you're planning on saving yourself until marriage. Good – keep it that way! It's hard because you may feel pressure from your peers and pressure from boyfriends, but so what! It's your body, not theirs. Lastly, I want to tell you that true love is loving yourself enough to fulfill your dreams. You haven't loved until you've loved yourself enough to go after the things you want out of life.

So dream big; don't be afraid to think outside the box.
Live fearlessly. Let that be your theme – "Live
Fearlessly." Don't be afraid to speak your thoughts.
Ask for what you really want. Don't be afraid of success.
Don't be afraid to give, and don't be afraid to receive.
Life is so much bigger than you can even image – it has
the whole world to offer.
I love you and God does too!

Sincerely
Shavonna

෨෩

Shavonna Cole, Founder & CEO of Nurture Over Nature, NFP,
has dedicated over a decade of her life to mentoring teens.
Attaining a Bachelor of Science in Psychology from Western
Illinois University along with her personal and career
experience inspired her to develop an advice column strictly
for youth; www.dearvonna.com. Shavonna also works in
Chicago, IL as a Prevention Specialist and Mentor
Coordinator, where she uses positive youth development to
help prevent teens against drug use.

෨෩

Dyana Williams

Radio Host + Life Coach

Dearest Dyanita,

So much lies ahead of you. Yours will be a fulfilling and blessed journey. Having used my time machine, I've come back to you at a critical period to share some insights about your future. Even at 16, you're fairly mature and focused about your purpose. Thank goodness that you have nurturing and encouraging parents who have instilled in you a love for Almighty God, family, friends and community. Their lesson that "anything the mind can conceive and believe, you can achieve" will be a guiding inspiration for you forever. Always honor your mother, Nancy, and father, George, as they will be your biggest supporters and closest friends.

It's a good thing that you are a goal oriented person who also journals. This way you have an outlet for your thoughts and feelings.

Also, you can document your life as it unfolds. Setting goals and ongoing five year plans will keep you on point with aspirations. Having a plan will lead you to the success that you will enjoy the majority of your life. You won't be afraid to work hard; in fact, you'll be rather determined to win and have a balanced life. You will be highly respected by your employers, colleagues, family, friends and the community at large. Incredible professional and personal opportunities will flow your way all the time!

Education and learning will be the mandate of your life. While you go to City College in New York for one year, then leave to pursue a career as a radio and television personality, it will take you over twenty years to get your bachelor's degree. The promise that you make to your professor mother to graduate from college will be a prideful day, especially since you will do so cum laude from Temple University with a degree in radio, television and film.

You are a giver. Become a bit more cautious about your generosity on every level. Exercise better judgment when it comes to how and who you give to.. Not everyone is as kind, thoughtful and caring as you are. Be very mindful of that. I know that your parents' divorce as well as your breakup with a man who you deeply loved will be a sorrow that you carry forever. Remember that a broken heart can mend, and you will love again. You will meet some fascinating men, but keep in mind that some relationships have an expiration date while others are meant to be with you for the rest of your life.

Dyana, never lose sight of the relationship you have with yourself. Many times in pursuit of being loved by someone else, we overlook our self esteem. Constantly read and listen to things that will fortify you. Associate with like minded positive people who are about something. Cultivate an inner circle of trustworthy people who will be honest, care about you and truly love you for you. Dee Dee, don't lose sight of the little girl in you. Play with your dolls, laugh, smile, dance...have fun, lots of it, especially as you get older. Life is filled with adventures and adversities. You will meet both with enthusiasm and courage.

Being an only child will prepare you well for the ability to enjoy your own company. It will also cause you to forge strong, meaningful and lasting relationships with friends who become part of your extended family. Indulge in those things that bring you joy. Reading, cinema, vintage dolls, art, memorabilia, and traveling the globe will enhance your life in an amazing way.

As a radio and television personality, you will use your voice to educate and entertain millions. Embrace your role as a natural born leader, but know when to follow. Continue to concentrate on leaving a legacy to enhance the lives of others. Making a difference and serving the community via the media and the non-profit that you establish will be a priority to you. Donate, volunteer, tithe, and encourage others to do the same.

The most important undertaking that you'll be involved in will be child rearing. As a mother, you will have two sons, (Caliph & Salahdeen) and a daughter, (Princess Idia). Through various tribulations and triumphs, they will teach you the true meaning of love.

Being a parent doesn't come with a manual (although many times you will wish you had one!). On the job training is what you'll get, but you will learn as you go. Remember your grandmother's approach and the advice your mother has given you. It will make things so much better.

Dyana, the spirit of your ancestors remains with you where ever you go. Cherish and celebrate them, as you have inherited generations of wonderful people. Please receive each day as if it were your last and live it to the fullest. Allow your mistakes to become lessons that you grow from and never stop soaring!

Much Love,
Dyana

Dyana Williams' career exceeds limitation. Whether showcasing her talents in broadcasting, print journalism and community activism or television producing & reporting, life coaching and lecturing, she's remained a constant force in the entertainment industry for over three deades. Currently, Williams hosts "Soulful Sunday," a weekly show broadcast via Radio One adult contemporary station, WRNB-FM, which won the Achievement in Radio Award for Best Weekend Show in Philadelphia for 2006 and has been nominated every year since. Each Sunday, 10am to 3pm, she can be found at 107.9 on the FM dial (and RNBPHILLY.COM) where she deftly weaves vintage sounds from Motown to Stax to The Sound of Philadelphia, along with compelling interviews. Ever mindful of the importance of family, Williams is most proud of her role as mother to her three children, Salahdeen, Princess Idia and Caliph, from her former union with acclaimed Rock and Roll Hall of famer producer/songwriter, Kenny Gamble.

Sandra Payne

Film Producer + Writer

Dear Sandy,
More than 30 years
have passed since we've
last seen each other. In
that time, I've learned
so many lessons —some
of them from you. I
wish I could share my
hard-won knowledge with you to ease your journey, but
I know you're on the path that got me here, so I'm reluc-
tant to say too much. I'm not interested in a do-over. I
wouldn't be the woman I am today without the life you
and I have lived.

Still, if I could wrap my arm around your shoulder and
whisper a little wisdom in your ear, it would be this: love
yourself. You're worthy. You're good. You're enough. I
say this because I know from the perspective of time
that you didn't appreciate the many gifts you had
because you were so busy judging yourself, making
harsh comparisons and finding yourself lacking.

If only you could focus on what a miracle life is, you wouldn't waste a second of it choosing to feel like a "less than." Eleanor Roosevelt once said, "No one can make you feel inferior without your consent." The glaring truth in her statement is that it's your choice.

In reality, you are unique in time and space—an ephemeral snowflake fluttering around the world experiencing a range of cultures, destinations, events and people. Rest assured that you have a good heart. You are worthy of every good thing that has happened, and you are strong enough to withstand every tough situation to come. I know this with certainty because when I pause to look back, I can see the trail we made through the snow, and I'm so very grateful for our life.

Besides, like so many people, we've always done the best we could with the skills we had at the time. So go easy on yourself. You deserve love. Know this. Believe it. Live it. For armed with the love of self, there is no challenge that will be too daunting. And that hole in your heart—the one you've kept open to maintain the illusion that you're not enough—will close.

You will be whole. Your journey through life will shine because the knowledge that you are loved will come from within. It's the kind of light that has the power to lead others out of the darkness.

The Dutch have a proverb that says: "Love others well, but love thyself the most; give good for good, but not to thine own cost."

So, dear Sandy, erase the thought that your worth is less than someone else's. We are all equal. And the path that we walk is our own, so there is no need to compare or judge. Love yourself. You're worth it. And I thank you.

Love,
Sandy

Sandra J. Payne is an award-winning writer and filmmaker, as well as world traveler. Sandra was a staff writer for the children's television show, Barney & Friends, and now writes, directs and produces digital content. Within this realm, Sandra has worked on three different web series via her production company, SPwrite Productions. She was the director/producer of the interview talk show The Web.Files (51 episodes), writer/director/producer of the comedy web series Life with Kat & McKay (21 episodes), and currently directs and produces the comedy talk show, Ask Grim (8 episodes). As a freelance writer, Sandra also writes for several magazines. Most recently, she has written cover features and an etiquette column for Celeb Life magazine. She's interviewed many celebrities, including Kristen Bell, Armand Assante, Mike Rowe from Dirty Jobs, and Lisa Edelstein from House. She's also contributed a story that has been reprinted four times in the Chicken Soup for the Soul series. In her travels, she lived in Indonesia and Austria, spent two months in India, and has been to five continents around the world (so far!).

Aldeana Frazell

Founder + Editor, Soluv Magazine

Dearest Aldeana,

I'm writing to let you know that you did a great job of getting me where I am today. My message from the future is that you and all sixteen-year old women are heroines, with unique journeys leading to unique accomplishments. As heroines, you come furnished with an arsenal of tools, instruments, and allies. The key is consciously realizing that you already have what you need so that you can effectively use it for your highest potential.

One of your primary tools of empowerment comes in the form of intuition, also described as hunches, or just "I get this feeling that..." At the age of sixteen, freely test out your intuition. Make an intention to strengthen it to razor sharpness. Learn to listen to your hunches, to your feelings, and to your desires. You know a lot, let your intuition uncover it. The ability to trust your own intuition is the way to believe in yourself.

Proficiency in this area is the connection to healthy self worth and is how you become your own best friend. Nevertheless, you must always use your intuition with the compassionate tool of gentle self-forgiveness. Coupling intuition with tools of self-compassion is how you honor yourself and maintain a healthy self-worth.

The second item you already possess is your voice; use your voice to communicate healthy boundaries for yourself. Speaking up keeps you in tune with your preservation and bonded with your self-respect. During your day-to-day encounters, people and situations that make you feel uncomfortable will present themselves. Although these types of situations are a part of every person's life, it is not okay for another person to intentionally or unintentionally put you in a position where you feel unsafe physically or emotionally. It is your right to stand up against it. The greatest repellant for these occurrences is to acknowledge and state that your personal boundaries are crossed. Follow up this verbal acknowledgment by firmly stating that you want the uncomfortable behavior or situation stopped. Whether simple or complex, developing consistent healthy boundary setting is a process of self growth.

The only way to effectively develop it is to put it into practice as situations requiring its use arise.

Life comes with unexpected rewards and challenges. Know that everyone encounters feelings of fear in the form of uncertainty and inadequacy. Fear crops up as an opponent many times and in different disguises during your journey. If you sense that fear is filling your mind and taking over your confidence, know that there is no error in retreat.

Knowing when to retreat is a tool from your intelligence. Use moments of retreat as a time to seek God's spiritual guidance. Spiritual guidance is your ally and is always with you whether you see it or not. Through prayer or meditation, stay in touch with your guidance and consult Him on a regular basis. The key to utilizing this powerful ally is being open to hearing and accepting the answers given. Spiritual answers come in different and numerous ways. For example, you may hear guidance through your intuition or in the caring words of a parent. Your answer may be in the book a friend recommends or in the presentation of an opportunity. Just be open, listen, hear, and accept the answer given. Your spiritual experiences include unanswered prayers containing fervent requests for specific relationships, jobs, and desired opportunities. Make the best effort you can to trust your guidance. I find that when I intentionally go against guidance and pursue what is deemed "Not for me" I encounter pain. On the other hand, when I yield and work through the disappointment of an unanswered prayer, I find that God's alternative is always greater than I can imagine. If for some reason you find that you did not listen to guidance, pull out your self-forgiveness and chalk it up to a lesson you needed to experience. Know that you always have God's spiritual guidance regardless of your choice to heed it in the immediate.

Armed with intuition as a tool, your voice as an instrument and God as an ally, your heroine journey can continue. These things are what you need in order to choose your blind turns with caution and celebrate your milestones with joyful abandon. To all the 16-year-old heroines, know you are made of great character and strength. There will be times when you will experience profound peace at the bottom of what can be described as one of your darker moments and have great discomfort and fear at the top of one your more popular successes. Remember there are no mistakes. Learn from your journey and teach from your experience.

Signed,
Aldeana Frazell

ഌൠ

Poised with an impressive resume, Aldeana's work experience includes working as an Internet Project Manager for Reed Communications & McGraw Hill Publishing. She has a BBA in Business from Georgia State University and an Associated Degree in Graphic Design from the UCLA Extension program. Aldeana went on to accept a design position at a California spiritual center called Agape. Utilizing her connections at both the Agape Spiritual Center and Impact Personal Safety, she went out and interviewed professionals dedicated to fueling the power of self-esteem. While doing these interviews, she was able to create a team of writers that included not only herself, but seasoned professional with vast backgrounds. With the combination of project management and design skills, Aldeana is able to create the powerful magazine Soluv, supporting the Truth that all Women are Beautiful.

ഌൠ

Sarah Cook

Founder, Raising CEO Kids

Dear Sarah,
I'm sitting on my favorite couch
with my laptop resting on my
knees and a delicious bar of my
favorite chocolate with chili
peppers right by my side. I have
so much to tell you! I shall start with that which has
brought me the most soul-searching and heartache over
the years – perfection. Sweet Sarah, you don't have to
be perfect. Life is about striving, going the distance,
falling short at times, and sometimes letting go all
together. It's not about what "they" think of you or
what "they" expect of you. It's about living with passion
and the excellence you define. Life is about finding joy
in little things and cherishing relationships – especially
the one with yourself. Love you for who you are. As I
have learned to love me, I have found that I am talented, that I have gifts to share, and that what I do does
make a difference in the world. As you invest in learning
to love and embrace yourself, I know you will find the

same things. I have done many things in the years since I was your age to learn to love and get along with myself. Some of my favorites have been keeping a gratitude journal, writing affirmations on the bathroom mirror, keeping company with people that uplift me, and taking time to be quiet. I remember that I lied to myself when I was your age, telling myself that I didn't have time to do any of those silly things. Don't listen to the lies! You deserve great friends, quiet time, and loads of affirmations!

Sarah, embrace money and learn to master it. Money is not evil and it can't buy happiness, but it does provide choices. Learning to stretch a dollar, balance your checkbook, protect your credit score, live well below your paycheck, give abundantly to others, and enjoy some money for yourself are all things I wish I had learned before I was out of high school. There is nothing to fear with money. Get comfortable with it! Fill your life with adding value to others, and you will find that life will reward you well.

I want you to know that I have found freedom in speaking up and standing for what I believe in rather than hiding in the shadows of life. Yes, you will be subject to the criticism of others, but you will also be a light that others will look to for hope and courage when they have lost their way.

Day to day tasks always had a way of killing my joy until I made a game out of them. I now play Tetris with the dishwasher, climb Mt. Laundry, and listen to music as I make things sparkle and gleam. Challenge yourself to find joy in everyday tasks or set aside the money to delegate them to someone else!

Sarah, I hope you will never stop dreaming, always keep learning, trust God, and take that trip to Europe! The experience will be something you will treasure for a lifetime.

Hugs from the future,
Sarah

Sarah Cook, Founder of Raising CEO Kids, knows first-hand what it is like to grow up in an entrepreneurial home and the benefits that it can bring to kids. Sarah received her BA in Family Studies from Utah State University and has owned a successful nation-wide direct sales skin care business for 17 years. In the last two years Sarah has worked diligently with her three children to help bring their business ideas to life. During this time she also interviewed over 150 successful young entrepreneurs from around the world. Now she freely shares what she has learned with others.

Jennifer Sarpong

Author + Life Coach

Dear 16 year old Jennifer,
First of all, I need you to know and totally be convinced of these three things:

1) You are loved
2) You matter
3) You can make a difference.

Yes, even with your so called "flaws" you are of such great value. Your worth is not determined by what you've done (good or bad). It's determined by who you are. And you, girlfriend, are a child of God. That means your worth is unimaginably high. I wish I could give you a picture of how much you're loved. It's deep. Not like those superficial "I love you's" that you hear your girlfriends mention sometimes when talking about the guy they have the latest crush on. It's also not like that conditional love that you see in the movies or on TV. God's love for you is 100% steady and unchangeable. So you can stop "doing things" just to prove your worth to everyone or trying to get people to like or love you.

That's like fighting for something you already have. Don't make yourself a slave to the expectations of other people anymore. Don't change yourself in an attempt to fit in with others. You now officially have permission to be 100% authentically you. Eventually, the rough edges will be worked out on their own.

Your life is going to be a masterpiece created one stroke at a time. It's ok if the entire picture doesn't make sense yet. You are a paintbrush in the hands of the world's greatest Artist! Some of the strokes you've experienced so far may have been dark and full of pain; others are light and full of fun, joy, and excitement. All of these changes and moves can sometimes be confusing. Sometimes you don't know whether your life is making a straight line or going in circles. Relax and enjoy who you are now and where you are now, while on the way to becoming what you want to be. Don't let fear steal the joy and excitement of this amazing time in your life. There are a lot of "firsts" going on for you right now, and that can be a little scary. But that's ok. Have fun, make mistakes, learn, and don't take yourself so seriously.

Cry when you need to and laugh when you want to; even if you're the only one who thinks something is funny. Be angry when you're angry. Just allow yourself to feel, breathe, and be 100% alive, no matter what people around you may think. You're beautifully unique, and the world needs to see that. While everyone around you is busy pretending to be something that they're not, your sincerity will be a huge breath of fresh air to so many people.

The things you don't like about yourself and the things that you feel are "strange" or "quirky" about your personality, body, and family are the things that make you so irreplaceable and extraordinary! Never be ashamed of who you are; you are a one of a kind masterpiece. And please remember this: You are an original so don't waste anymore time trying to be a copy of your friends or family. Learn more about what makes you tick. What makes you happy? What makes you sad? Do the things you truly enjoy, even if you have to do them by yourself. If you make mistakes, so what?! It's not the end of the world. If some people don't like you, so what?! There are plenty of other people in the world

world who will love you….the real you. Making mistakes means that you're taking chances and growing. That's a good thing because it means you are alive; you're HUMAN.

You've got one life to live. God loves you. You've been blessed with so many gifts and talents. The ball of life is in your court, so you have nothing to lose and everything to gain. Just go for it! And if you fall, get back up again. Smile. Dream. Love. Be confident by doing the things you've been scared to do for so long. However, make sure you take the advice and wisdom of adults you trust on the journey with you.

Life is not meant to be cautiously and fearfully survived, it is meant to be lived!! So live without fear. You were made for this.

Love,
Jennifer

ഇ‌ാ‌ര

Jennifer Sarpong is the founder and creator of the
top-ranked website help-my-self-esteem.com. She is an
author, life coach, social entrepreneur, and motivational
speaker who touches hearts and changes lives
internationally. Her style is engaging, thought-provoking and
down-to-earth as she tackles the issues that keep people
from being successful and discovering their true identity and
worth. The goal of Jennifer's life is simple — to lead, uplift,
and inspire people to reach their full potential by using their
God-given gifts and abilities to change their world.

ഇ‌ാ‌ര

Lisa Steadman

Business Coach

Dear Lisa,
I know there's a lot going
on in your life right now. I
know things FEEL big, bad,
and overwhelming. I know
you're scared about the
future. I know you're
hurting. And I'm sorry.
The truth is that you don't deserve what's happening
right now. It's not your fault. What's happening
between your parents is not your fault. I'm sorry they
dragged you into the middle of it. Their struggles, both
financial and personal, are affecting you, but it's not
your fault. The good news is that they eventually
overcome both, so there are plenty of happy times
ahead for your family. Hang in there! I know you're
struggling to make a big decision about the next year of
your life, and it feels unfair to be put in this position. It
would be so much easier if you could be a "normal"

teenager and not have to make such grownup decisions like who you want to live with, or where you want to go to school. The truth is that there's no such thing as "normal" so stop trying to be normal and start celebrating the smart, special, beautiful girl you already are! When I say the word "beautiful," I know you don't believe me. Lisa, it's true. And here's another truth. You need help healing your body story. It's not that your body isn't beautiful. It's that you can't see or feel or understand its beauty. So let me say it again.

YOU ARE BEAUTIFUL.

And again. You are beautiful.

If you need help healing your body, please get it. And don't ask Mom. Ask Dad. He will help you. I promise! Healing your body story now will save you years of pain and anguish. You deserve to have help. You can't do it alone right now. That's okay. Ask for help. This is about you. It's time to love YOU. It's time to start loving yourself for the brilliant, creative, imaginative, smart, sensitive, intuitive, compassionate young woman that you are right now. These gifts serve you well in the future.

Lisa, your future is so much bigger and better than the life you're living today. I know you know that. I know that's what keeps you going in the hard times. I know sometimes you wonder how you know what you know. God wasn't kidding around when he gave you the wisdom he did before you were born. Trust that innate wisdom. It will never steer you wrong.

This is all truly wonderful. However, the most wonderful part of your life has nothing to do with your external accomplishments. It has to do with the love you discover and cultivate. You have your whole life ahead of you. It is a wonderful life to look forward to! You do brilliant things in the world. You write books. And get on TV. And make a lot of money. And buy your own home. People admire and respect you.

After lots of fun dating adventures, you meet the most extraordinary man who loves you, supports you, celebrates you, thinks you're beautiful, and wants nothing more than for you to be YOU. He is the love you want now, and he is worth the wait! Don't give up when he doesn't show up right away. And don't settle for those infuriating boys who just don't "get" you.

Not only do you find the love of your life, but you start loving yourself and honoring who you are on such a deep level. You actually LOVE yourself and your life. Amazing!

Be patient, Lisa. Life gets a whole lot better. If I could offer you one final piece of advice, it is this. Start loving yourself NOW. Turn down the volume on your self-criticism, judgment, shame, and blame. There is nothing wrong with you. You are not screwed up, a failure, or unworthy of being loved. I love you so much. I'm proud of you. And I want you to know I'm always here for you.

xoxo,
Lisa Marie Steadman

Lisa Steadman is an internationally acclaimed best-selling author, sought after speaker, results coach, and CEO of Woohoo, Inc. As Chief Woohoo Woman, Lisa loves collaborating with entrepreneurs, experts, authors, fellow Woohoo Women, and even Fortune 500 companies to build buzz-worthy brands, create compelling online communities and fan bases, and leverage one's leadership into a purposeful, passionate, and prosperous platform.

Kendra Kabasele

Journalist

Dear Teen Kendra,

You are right.

You know the days when you sit on your bed and look out the window at the grand, towering, poplar tree in your front door neighbors' backyard? You know that persistent thought and that nagging feeling you feel whenever you look at it and imagine, 'There has *got* to be so much more out there beyond this tree'? You're right. There is a whole world waiting for you, beyond that tree and beyond the comfortable, and familiar, suburban neighborhood you grew up in and love, even beyond the countless footsteps you've taken around your birth city, Montreal. There is *even* a whole world beyond that, a place in which you will learn more, love more, and *live* more. So keep that in mind whenever you gaze at that tree. Know that there are places you have yet to see, people you have yet to meet, and yes, dreams you have yet to realize.

You will see, as you embark on life's journey into the unknown, that while you may feel unsure or even indecisive at times, you *are* equipped with the tools from your upbringing that you require for your journey. Now, don't get me wrong. There are new tools you will pick up along your journey as well. There will be pieces of yourself that you will discover along the way. There are so many life lessons I could impart on you; so many things that you will learn in life. Some of those lessons would not serve the same purpose if I tell you all about them. Telling you about every detail of every experience may jeopardize the mystique, challenge, and, most importantly, the impact and lesson of each experience. The best way I can express this to you, based on my experience, is to keep doing what you are doing in continuing to be who you are! As long as you stay true to your core values and morals, some of the challenging things you encounter in life will deflect off of you like menacing objects off of a protective shield. Now, I never thought I would have to warn you about these things, because when I was your age, I may have been slightly naïve in thinking that as long as I was nice to others, they would be nice to me.

Well, in theory, that sounds good, but let me warn you - this is not always the case. I am here to warn you that when you cross paths with people who treat you poorly, you need to stand up for yourself. I've seen it, so I want you to be ready. There will be people who will try to take advantage of your skills. People will also take advantage of your kindness, and mistake it for weakness; there will even be people who will treat you poorly out of ignorance. I remember one time, just after Journalism school, I was working at a magazine. There was an employee there who discriminated against me by mocking my ethnic background and my dad's country of origin. Boy, did I set him straight! And then, something unexpected happened. I found out, moments after it occurred, that my immediate boss had told Human Resources what had just happened! I didn't even have to say anything! They told me that my boss had witnessed everything and that I could file a complaint if I wanted to. Of course, I did, because of the principle. There will be ignorance in the world, but there will also be goodness. This story demonstrates both sides.

I can tell you that you will not have all of the answers in life, but that you can seek them. I know you, and I know how curious you are by nature. I know you wonder about things, worry about others and even think of others before yourself. These are all great qualities to have as long as you don't allow people to take advantage of you. As you continue to grow, change, learn and see new parts of the world, your interests may change and even become more clear, with those experiences. Some outlooks you have now will end up maturing, while other positions you stand for may take a 180 degree turn. I can tell you that love, no matter what type, will have many lessons for you. Love will bring you surprises; good and bad. You may think you know everything about it. Well, love, as it relates to life, can throw you curveballs. It can reveal things about others to you just as much as it can show you exactly who you are. It has a way of making you celebrate and at times feel disappointed, sometimes as a result of your expectations or selflessness. Sometimes, well, just because. And so, I stand by my word that some things you will be experiencing in life and in your promising future, are better off left unmentioned, by me, your older self. You will thank me once you get here. In my mid-twenties, I made it a point that I was going to be optimistic about the ups and downs I knew I was going to endure whenever I was starting a new chapter. You will be thankful that you get to appreciate the surprises, challenges, triumphs and disappointments. If I told you about some of those now, I would not be doing any justice to the character we are building for you. Once you catch up to the age I am now, you will be able to say that you were well-prepared for the journey. Your transition from teenage Kendra to adult Kendra will remain authentic as we not only keep striving to build upon our character, but as we wait to hear from our elderly self, with the next words of wisdom. (smile)

Love,
Kendra

ॐ

Kendra Kabasele grew up in Montreal, in the heart of Canada's cultural crossroads. She developed her love of communication and the arts in this vibrant, cosmopolitan city that is rich with the linguistic and cultural influences of its international populace. Kendra earned a BSc. in Psychology and a Graduate Diploma in Journalism from Concordia University. After moving to Los Angeles, Kendra quickly became acclimated and became very involved in the entertainment and media scene. From working in the marketing department of KCET Television (PBS) to assisting in production for one of the 2005 Los Angeles mayoral debates and for the 2005 NAACP Image Awards, Kendra has already worked in a range of areas in media and television in Los Angeles. Kendra just wrapped up working at Corbis, one of the top photo licensing agencies in the world, where she worked as a leading Senior Account Executive in Media, overseeing the placement, distribution and licensing of the agency's photography and film footage. She was in charge of licensing to television and film studios, magazines, newspapers, and other media outlets.

Jess Berger

Teen Life Coach

Dear 16 Year Old Jess, YOU ROCK. (Cue your eye roll here...) I know, a bit cheesy. But seriously, sometimes it's difficult to give yourself credit for all that you do. I've learned how crucial it is to take stock of your hard work and acknowledge yourself for your successes. From piles of homework to acting classes, from sports teams to community service projects, you are overloaded and overworked. To keep from burning out, you must stop, reflect and give yourself a giant pat on the back. I promise, it is neither egotistical nor selfish to do so. Rather, it deepens your self-awareness and honors some of your deepest core values: productivity, accomplishment, and integrity. So go ahead, say it out loud and own it! YOU ROCK.

Cut your parents some slack. Did I really just say that?! After all of the battles about boys and curfews and parties and boys and driving...yes, I encourage you to cut your parents some slack. Just because they are adults does not make them perfect. It's easy to forget that being a parent does not mean that suddenly you have it all figured out. Your parents are human. Just like you, they make mistakes. Just like you, they are doing the best they can with the tools they've been given. And just like you, they need some extra slack every now and again. Looks fade, but your body is forever. In a society that's obsessed with attaining the perfect body, it's easy to get caught in the swirling tornado of fad diets, excessive exercising and poor body image. But your body is so much more than just a shell. Your body allows you to run in your sports games and dance at the prom and rock out at concerts and hug your friends and go after your wildest dreams! So don't take it for granted. Instead of comparing yourself to others, instead of obsessing over 5 pounds, instead of depriving your body of a healthy lifestyle- be *grateful* for it!!

The truth is your looks will fade, but your body is with you for the rest of your life. So be good to it. Take care of it. And thank your lucky stars every day to be healthy.

Ask for help. Often. Let's cut to the chase: asking for help does not mean you're weak, stupid, helpless, incompetent or lame. Asking for help means you are wise enough to know your limitations, and you are brave enough to seek out the support that will allow you to achieve your greatest potential. Trying to keep all of your balls in the air without asking for help is exhausting and a waste of energy. I promise, no one will think less of you for acknowledging the truth: no single person can accomplish great things alone. So start asking for what you need. Everyone, yes everyone, will rise up to support you. Get perspective- this too shall pass! From nasty rumors, to public breakups, to mean girls and cliques, high school is full of painful stuff. In the moment, the drama can feel so huge that it's hard to see the light at the end of the tunnel. But the truth is that the challenges you face don't *define* you, they *shape* you. They make you a better friend, a stronger individual and a more compassionate human being. So stay positive.

Keep your chin up. And remember, this too shall pass! Lastly, as Nana used to say, Live. Love. Laugh.

In love and gratitude,
Jess

Jessica Rae Berger is a certified Teen Wisdom™ Coach and certified Professional Career Coach based in Los Angeles. After graduating Cum Laude from NYU, Jess traveled from South America to Southeast Asia to absorb knowledge and insight into the world and its many cultures. After settling in LA, Jess felt in her heart it was time to start giving back to the community in a significant way. Life coaching for teens became her path towards that goal, as she is deeply committed to empowering teens to truly value themselves as insightful, powerful and confident young people. Jess is currently pursuing a Masters in Counseling Psychology, and continues to affect lasting, positive change on the lives of teens and their families.

Khia Thomas

Career Coach + Professor

Dear Khia,

You are more than smart. If there is only one single thing you know to be a true and absolute fact, it's that you are smart. For the majority of your life, being intelligent has seemed like a double-edged sword – it wins you praise from teachers but it also creates sneers from classmates for being the "teacher's pet." Those straight "A" report cards become big fat expectations that you feel you have to live up to for fear of whatever punishment is waiting if you came home with anything *less than*.

Right now, your smartness feels like your solitary badge of honor, your one-way ticket to a better education, your promise to a "better life," and one of the only things you can say absolutely definitively about yourself.

I am smart.

You instinctively know what Maya Angelou is talking about when she refers to "those pretty women." It is because deep down in your heart, you truly believe that you aren't one of them. The reason why is not because no one has ever told you so, but because of the multitude of voices who have told you otherwise that you take to heart as truth. These are the voices of strangers who fawn over the pretty sisters with long hair and light eyes. They are talking directly to your sisters – and not you. You feel invisible. And when you don't feel invisible, words like *fat* and *ugly* are hurled heavily like rocks, intended only to leave a wound. Looking from grown-up eyes, there are other voices that were well intentioned, but nevertheless they reinforce your worst fears about yourself. They confirm what everyone else is saying (or isn't saying) about you. "I'm just telling this to help you" sounds identical to "Let me cosign what everyone else has ever said about you. You *are* fat and ugly" to the sensitive soft-spoken child you are.

It hurts. Still.

Most sixteen year olds take a whole lot of flak for being defiant and mouthy and full-of-attitude. But you are not one of them. You don't yet have the vocabulary or confidence to not-so-politely tell these people to go screw themselves. And maybe it's not exactly lady-like to go around telling people to screw themselves, but all of the voices who ever told you that you were anything less than magnificent fully deserve to be told about themselves. However it comes out.

Tell 'em your thirty-year-old self told you it was perfectly acceptable.

You may not be able to see it right now, but there is much more to you than the quadratic equations and expository essays on "Turn of the Screw" and verb conjugation en Espanol that seem to make up the sum total of your life. You will love. It isn't so far off in the future that you will fall head-over-heels with a man who loves that you love books. He sings to you gorgeously off -key about your beautiful skin. You will have interesting conversations about everything under the sun – from your favorite college professor to having the courage to be yourself to your dumbest mistakes ever. You will emerge from underneath the cloak of invisibility you carried around with you all those years. When he says he loves you, you will hold onto those words and keep them tucked away to live in your heart. It is an affirmation that all those voices from the past were dead wrong.

You will finally feel more than smart. You will feel loveable.

You will later wonder if it was all a dream when heartbreak happens. Breaking up with your first love is never easy, but this will feel like a much deeper loss. It will feel like losing a part of a newfound identity. It will also feel like losing everything you ever wanted – someone to kiss, someone to share your innermost thoughts with, someone who sees the worst of you and loves you anyway. It will feel crushing and painful and defeating, but you will love and be loved again.

What you will come to know over time is that being loveable isn't situational. It doesn't exist or cease to exist based on being romantically involved with someone in your life. Love doesn't just exist in a shared moment of passion, but it also resides in everyday experiences with yourself like walking down the aisle in the grocery store.

All of those trophies and certificates you have been given are great for show. They make your parents feel proud. They look great on display on the mantelpiece. These tokens do not even come close to affirming the whole of you. Neither will a man or some magic weight on the scale that you could reach if only you were to portion control and exercise yourself down to half your size. Bending over backwards to get people to like you and recognize you and *love you* won't work either.

You will find out that you are loveable when you're fat or when you're skinny, when you're at your worst or your best, when you're feeling down or on top of the world. It is a big fat lie that love is a condition of whether you are or you aren't [fill in the blank for whatever imaginary clause you attach to being loved]. As long as you're living and breathing, you're capable and worthy of experiencing love.

Besides these lessons about love, one of the biggest things you fail to realize about yourself is that you are *talented*. Among one of your God-given talents is the ability to craft and bend and shape-shift the written word into *art*. All of those hours upon hours spent devouring every single word crammed inside worn paperback books will turn out to be one of your strongest assets. All of those hours in your twelve and thirteen-year-old life when you were determined to write the new Babysitters' Club – a version a little more relevant to your day-to-day life experiences – were not in vain. You had no way of knowing this at the time, but all of those minutes and hours are leading up to your own distinctive brand of artfully maneuvering the written word.

Take ownership of the fact that you are a creative. Over the years you will write millions of words – some for personal benefit, others for assignments, and still others as deliverables to your job. There is one common thread through it all: You strive to make every single one of these tasks read like the next great American masterpiece. You see little bits of genius in everyday speech and lines from your favorite hip hop songs that inspire you to be a better writer. Your in-born creativity deserves to be nurtured and honed and mastered just like your intellect. Your words, your thoughts don't just belong on pieces of paper tucked away in your private journal. On that sheet of paper, you have embraced those uncomfortable thoughts and parts of yourself – that for better or worse – make you who you are. If only one person in the whole wide world were to understand and feel where you were coming from in that intimate moment when you poured your soul out on paper, then you have made a major accomplishment to be proud of. You have stood true to yourself so that others can feel you. You have fully embraced being *you*.

You are the same person at sixteen that you will be at thirty with a little more wisdom, life experience, and understanding of yourself. You will continue to be slightly socially awkward with a silly sense of humor. You may still be shy with new people, but you'll be amazingly friendly and open once you have established a connection. Continue to process your thoughts deeply before you speak. You may not take ownership of it right now, but you are much more than smart. You may relate more to the Ugly Duckling than the beautiful swan. You may not ever be voted most popular in anyone's superlative contest. There may be people who will mistreat you or tear your heart into teeny-tiny pieces.

You deserve to explore your life beyond what can be found in a textbook or what can be accomplished inside the walls of a university classroom, or later still, within the confines of a corporate office.

You are beautiful and loved and talented. When you listen to your heart and what you know to be true about yourself, you are living in brilliance.

Go forth and be brilliant.

Love,
Khia

Khia Ashanti Thomas, Ph.D., is still constantly reminding herself that she is more than just a "smart girl." Khia currently teaches at the university level and also enjoys a career as a writer, blogger, coach and entrepreneur. She earned a Ph.D. in Developmental Psychology from the University of Michigan in 2009. She spends her Saturdays developing the prototype for a dynamic coaching business, Your Grad School Coach, designed to demystify the graduate school admissions process and help applicants develop a winning game plan to get into the graduate program of their choice.

Lisa Nicole Bell

Author + Filmmaker + Entrepreneur

Dearest Lisa,
You represent endless opportunity. You're a vessel of light and possibilities, but you don't realize it yet. You have a hunch that you're supposed to do something great so just follow it. The journey is a long and winding one, so commit to success no matter how long it takes or what you have to overcome. Allow your intuition to guide you to where you belong.

Self-love and acceptance are essential to success as a woman. No matter what anyone says or does, be your own best friend. Give yourself whatever you believe you need from other people. Set aside any neediness to be liked because as you go through life, some people will simply not like you, and they won't always have a good reason. That's okay.

Don't obsess over fitting in with certain groups because the very things that keep you from fitting in are the same things that will make you loved and admired in the future. Let rejection motivate you to keep moving forward. Never take it personally. The best revenge is a life well lived so stay focused on what's most important. Take extra love, extra joy, and extra energy with you everywhere you go. Use it to make the ordinary world an extraordinary experience. Maintain a strong prayer life; God will be the air you breathe and the light on your path. No one will ever love you more deeply, unconditionally, and authentically as God. Your spiritual evolution will explode as you explore what God means to you. Allow it. Ralph Waldo Emerson says that God enters every individual through a private door. Don't allow other people to dictate the truth about your understanding and experience of God. A denomination, church, or preacher is much too small to contain your idea of God. Trust that as you pray for guidance, the way will unfold in front of you. Take every step with faith and confidence. Say no to the good so that you can say yes to the great. Your personal power will lie in your choices. You are the architect of your life.

Avoid playing the victim or believing that you're helpless. You can always start where **you are and change where you're going. Never** feel guilty for being who you are, saying what you feel, or doing what you believe is right.

Close the gap between the time you think of an idea and the time you take action. This will separate you from the talkers and speed your ascension to new heights. Do work you love that creates a meaningful legacy. Know that security is mostly an illusion, and that you and God are the only things that you can ever know for sure. Just because something is obvious to you doesn't mean it's obvious to the world. Test your assumptions. Try things. Stay curious, and stay in motion. Nurse your muse; if you don't, it will leave you.

Your relationships are one the most important indicators of how successful you'll be. If you ever want to take the temperature of your life, just look at the people around you and the relationships you have with them. Learn to set and honor boundaries. You have the good fortune of having an amazing father; continue to cherish him the way you do now.

Your relationship with him will anchor you as you become a woman. Choose men who have something to give you – love, resources, time, attention, and happiness. Be what you want to attract in a mate. Never accept poor treatment and ex-communicate toxic, abusive people. Remember that when you settle for less than you deserve, you'll get less than you settled for. You're gorgeous, smart, funny, and ambitious. Only accept the best in your life; this includes the people you allow to occupy your space.

The more self-sufficient you become, the happier you will be. This doesn't mean that you should ignore or eliminate the important people in your life. It means that you don't want your self-esteem tied to another person's opinion of you. You're a smart girl; own your brilliance and power. It's not necessary to internalize other people's issues and opinions. Sometimes you'll be sad, sometimes you'll be overjoyed, sometimes you'll be angry. Allow yourself to feel everything you feel, but always respond in ways that reflect integrity, honor, and respect.

Be willing to let go of what's familiar in order to explore the possibilities. Be clear about your vision and goals but remain flexible and open to new opportunities.

I'm so excited for you and the woman you're becoming. As Ralph Waldo Emerson (your soon-to-be favorite philosopher) says, "Do not go where the path may lead. Go instead where there is no path and leave a trail."

I love you.

Lisa

Lisa Nicole Bell is a social change agent, filmmaker, author and entrepreneur. As the CEO of Inspired Life Media Group, Lisa and her team use media to create positive change for the masses. Lisa has been featured in dozens of media outlets including Forbes, Huffington Post, Under 30 CEO, the Los Angeles Business Journal, and American Entertainment magazine.

About the Publisher

The Legacy Letters is published by Inspired Girls International, a subsidiary of Inspired Life Media Group. Inspired Girls creates content and programming for organizations across the world. From after school programs to television shows, Inspired Girls is a premier multimedia company that works alongside doctors, therapists, thought leaders, life coaches, girls, parents, and experts to create actionable content for young women. Learn more about Inspired Girls at www.inspiredgirlsonline.com.

About the Editor

Lisa Nicole Bell is a media personality, author, filmmaker, and entrepreneur. She uses all forms of media to create positive change and advance the social agenda. As the CEO of Inspired Life Media Group, Lisa guides her team as they build projects that are socially conscious and economically viable. Lisa and her work have been featured in publications such as American Entertainment magazine, Huffington Post, American Express Open, Under 30 CEO, Forbes, Honey magazine, and more. Learn more about Lisa and her upcoming projects at www.lisanicolebell.com.

NOTES + QUOTES

CPSIA information can be obtained at www.ICGtesting.com
Printed in the USA
BVOW02s1036161013

333906BV00001B/130/P